The Seven Albums

of Stovepipe

Paul H. Lepp

Copyright © 2024 Paul H. Lepp

ISBN (Hardback):   979-8-89381-060-8
ISBN (Paperback):   979-8-89381-061-5
ISBN (eBook):   979-8-89381-062-2

All rights reserved. No part of this book
may be reproduced or transmitted in any form or by any
means, electronic or mechanical, including photocopying, recording,
or by any information storage and retrieval system, without
permission in writing from the copyright owner.

The views expressed in this work are solely
those of the author and do not necessarily reflect the views of the
publisher, and the publisher hereby disclaims any
responsibility for them.

508 West 26th Street KEARNEY, NE 68848
402-819-3224
info@medialiteraryexcellence.com

Contents

Save Your Strength

Origin: Akron, Ohio
Year: 1968
Albums produced: 500

Bagpipes & Bongos

Origin: Columbus, Oh
Year: 1969
Albums produced: 500

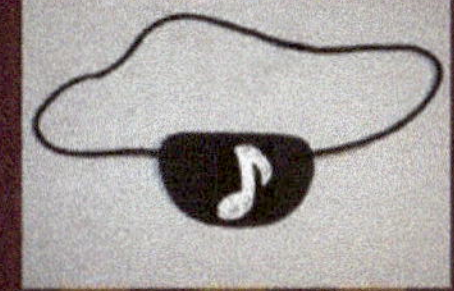

Atomic Peanut

Origin: Oh Rt. 33 (Ernie's
Full Service Garage)
Year: late 1969 - early 1970
Albums produced: 500

Radio Ventriloquist

Origin: Lancaster, Ohio
Year: 1970
Albums produced: 500

Sticks to Bricks

Origin: Sandusky, Ohio
/ Canadien Border
Year: 1971, 1972 (?)
Albums produced: 500

Good Wood

Origin: Cleveland, Ohio
(Museum of Art)
Year: 1973
Albums produced: 500

Pipe Reloaded or Bloodstream

is a compact disc said to
be made by Stovepipe (7
y rs before the
introduction of the CD in
1982)

Dedication

This book is dedicated to everyone who has never had a book dedicated to them. You now have this going for you…

Paul H. Lepp

Acknowledgment

To everyone I've crossed paths with, friend or foe, this work is as much yours as mine...

The Collector

I might not own all the information, but I do own most of the artifacts. Every great turning point in history leaves behind some artifact of the moment. With time, they become as important as the moment itself: proof. I find the period beginning with the end of World War II fascinating. It marks the start of the Boomer generation, born between 1945 and 1963, and their impact on the world.

Technology began advancing at a pace that outstripped our ability to comprehend it. Space became the new frontier for the Boomers, driven by the rapid advancement of technology. The development of space exploration has always been rapid and has had both positive and negative consequences.

Consider for a moment: twelve years after the atomic bomb, the Russians put up a satellite (a man-made star); twelve years after that, Americans put a man on the moon. Most born in 1945 caught it all before their twenty-fifth birthday. If you're like me, I caught it before my twenty-first. Boomers are the first to experience what other generations talked about — the weapons of mass destruction are here, we can move faster than the speed of sound, we've been to the moon.

For the Boomers, it's been about understanding the power of technology, the ability to launch rockets into space, but also the potential to unleash destruction. We can put space capsules on rockets or warheads on missiles, all with the push of a button. This dual nature of technology is a side effect of the Last Frontier. We're still in a period where we don't know if this side effect will overtake us or if we'll be able to control it. The artifacts are the footprints of this period, leading to an outcome of either exploration or annihilation. Boomers are the first generation to live in a world they're capable of destroying, and that makes them interesting.

Old money, well-invested from one generation to the next, has made me incredibly wealthy. I have more than I could ever spend in a lifetime. But wealth, in and of itself, holds little interest for me. The game of accumulating possessions and consuming more than anyone else pales in comparison to the pursuit of knowledge.

I overcame this boredom by starting to collect the artifacts behind the information. I have a carefully designed approach and a dedicated staff to implement my vision. They are experts in their field, equipped with cutting-edge technology, and I compensate them generously for their skills. They are highly skilled, capable of accessing information from a wide range of sources.

My collection encompasses artifacts from every major turning point and shift in direction experienced by the Boomers. My staff and I collaborate to identify potential acquisitions. Once a decision is made, we meticulously document the artifact, prioritizing its authenticity.

All major museums in this country are familiar with my staff, our approach, and my collection. They recognize the authenticity of my artifacts and acknowledge my status as a serious collector.

To illustrate the significance of my collection, consider this artifact: the lighter General Douglas MacArthur carried in his pocket during the Korean War in 1953, when President Harry Truman relieved him of command.

MacArthur's dismissal wasn't solely due to a breach of protocol, such as making the President land his plane first. Truman believed MacArthur was eager to escalate the conflict in Korea, a move that Truman felt the United States wasn't prepared for at the time.

The breach of protocol didn't go unnoticed. Truman, in a pointed remark, told MacArthur, "I don't care what you think of Harry Truman, the man, but I do care what you think of Harry Truman, the President." Their relationship deteriorated from that point forward.

His aides reported that the first thing MacArthur pulled from his pocket after his meeting with Truman was his lighter. It was a symbolic gesture, signifying the shift in power from the military to the civilian government. This was a pivotal moment in history, though I was only five years old at the time and my memories are hazy. But now, I possess that very lighter, a tangible reminder of that event.

The biggest drawback to MacArthur's plans was likely the revelation that Julius and Ethel Rosenberg had been convicted of passing atomic secrets to the Soviets. If the United States had maintained a technological advantage, MacArthur's strategy might have been viable. However, the Rosenberg case exposed the vulnerability of American security, triggering the arms race. I possess the shoes they wore to the electric chair, a chilling reminder of that era.

I was about six years old, in the late spring, when Senator Joe McCarthy launched his infamous accusations against officials in the Army, media, and other public figures, claiming they were communists. He fabricated these accusations, driven by his desire to gain political power.

I learned about political fabrication at an early age. During that spring, McCarthy's influence was so powerful that he managed to silence popular figures like Roy Rogers, Sergeant Joe Friday, and the Cisco Kid from evening television. Even at six years old, I could sense the danger he posed.

The American system faced a severe test during that period, but to its credit, no one with McCarthy's level of demagoguery has emerged since. I possess the microphone he used to spread his accusations, a chilling reminder of that era. It sits unplugged on a table in my office.

My collection includes the K-20 camera that was on the *Enola Gay*. I also have the keys Elvis used to unlock his shotgun two-room boyhood home in Tupelo, Mississippi. I even possess the belt Lee Harvey Oswald wore the day he shot President Kennedy and the cuff links Jack Ruby was wearing when he shot Oswald. I have starter pistols from every Olympic Games since the end of World War II, as well as Mickey Mantle's first and last car. I also own the bicycle that was stolen from the young Cassius Clay on his way to becoming Muhammad Ali. I even have the necktie Deep Throat wore on the day he revealed his identity, and the gavel that was used to announce the Roe v. Wade decision. These are just a few examples from my collection, but they give you a glimpse into the breadth and significance of the artifacts I possess.

These artifacts are just a few examples from my collection, which demonstrates the depth of my knowledge and expertise on this era. My evidence room is filled with artifacts, a testament to my deep involvement in the Military Industrial Complex. As a Boomer myself, my collection on this generation is constantly evolving and growing. My passion for this era drives my pursuit of these artifacts. Through years of experience, I've honed my skills and assembled a team that can identify pivotal moments in history and locate the artifacts that represent those turning points. For me, possessing these artifacts is like possessing a piece of history itself.

******

My staff recently uncovered some information that suggests we're missing a crucial turning point in our understanding of this era. It seems we're not as up-to-date as we thought. On July 20, 2012, during a routine review of inquiries and transactions on internet support platforms and search engines, my staff discovered an intriguing offer: 'Any record albums - made by Stovepipe - name your price.' The nine-word offer intrigued my staff for three reasons: the use of the term 'record album,' the name of the artist, and the open-ended price.

A quick search online reveals a wealth of information about the ten-inch, vinyl long play (LP) record album. This technology dominated the recording industry from about 1948 to 1982, when it was replaced by the compact disc (CD).

Record albums from this period also reflect a significant shift in American musical culture. For nearly two centuries, the piano had been the primary instrument in most homes. However, after World War II, the guitar rose to prominence, becoming the dominant instrument in American households. This shift marked a key turning point in the evolution of popular music.

Thirty-four years is a significant lifespan for any successful technology, especially considering the rapid pace of innovation experienced by the Boomer generation. This period is ten years longer than the time between the atomic bomb and the moon landing. For Boomers, the LP record album has always been a part of their lives. The advent of the CD relegated the LP to closets and attics, a change that occurred when the oldest Boomer was 37 and the youngest was 19. This shift marked the end of an era.

The LP record album is slowly fading into obscurity, a phenomenon that we, as Boomers, have overlooked in our rush to embrace new technologies. This is a testament to the rapid pace of innovation that has characterized our lives.

We acknowledge that our methods may have violated some privacy rules. We are prepared to face any fines or penalties for these actions. We can access your financial information, including your Social Security number and credit card details. We have access to your medical, legal, and military records. We know your blood type, cholesterol levels, social media posts, email addresses, and memberships in clubs and organizations. We can even access information about your family and friends. We can gather all this information in just fifteen seconds. We are not interested in your information or anyone else's, except for Stovepipe. We need to know more about this individual. To achieve our goal, we have begun to violate some rules, targeting the person who made the offer. This unconventional approach has yielded results.

While we know it's wrong, there's something about reading other people's emails that becomes addictive once you start. We've succumbed to this temptation, reading not only his emails but those of others as well. We've been captivated by the information we've found.

Since adopting this unconventional approach, my staff's progress reports have significantly expanded our understanding of the situation. We've determined that the person behind the offer is serious and not involved in any internet scams. He is employed by a group known as the 'Chronologists,' according to my staff. His real name is Thurmond Nogciewitzky, but he goes by the alias Thurston Nogwick.

This individual is a private investigator, operating under the name *'Python Private Investigators.'* His background check reveals a personality that seems tailor-made for an *avant-garde* foreign film – a character so unusual, it's almost impossible to understand. I've shared this observation with my staff, who simply respond with, 'I know,' and a knowing smile.

My staff has identified six individuals who have responded to the private investigator's online offer, representing about two percent of the total 247 hits. These individuals are now known to us as 'First Contacts.' We are monitoring all their correspondence.

While my staff finds amusement in the romantic emails exchanged by two of the 'First Contacts,' these individuals paint a surprisingly compelling picture of Stovepipe and his music. Interestingly, their background checks make the private investigator seem almost ordinary in comparison. I've shared this observation with my staff, who simply nod and smile in agreement.

My staff's investigation into the 'First Contacts' has occasionally led them down tangents, including discussions about sending a romantic email to one of the wives. I've made it clear that anyone involved in such activities will be immediately terminated.

While we'll cite ethical concerns, the real reason for terminating anyone involved in this behavior is that we need to stay focused on our mission of finding Stovepipe and his albums. We also need to maintain our perfect record of stealth, as any exposure could jeopardize our operation.

In all my years in this business, I've never encountered a group of individuals who have had such a strange effect on my staff as Thurston Nogwick and the First Contacts. My staff has yet to find any cyber footprints leading to the Chronologist, which is their current focus. However, it's clear that they are preoccupied with the unusual behavior of the First Contacts. When they presented me with the initial progress report, I noticed that their coffee breaks were becoming increasingly frequent, and their distraction with the First Contacts was becoming more apparent.

Each coffee break began with someone whispering the word 'maybe,' launching into a wide range of random topics. My staff indulged in these conversations, exploring ideas they wouldn't dare present in a formal report for fear of my scrutiny. These coffee breaks provided a much-needed outlet for their thoughts and anxieties.

Their 'maybe' conversations ranged from the hypothetical, like whether the South won the Civil War or if God is a woman, to the conspiratorial, like the true story behind Miss America 1950 or the possibility of a coin toss having more than two outcomes. They even explored the philosophical, pondering whether only spiritual people can swim or if libraries are the foundation of great democratic societies. They even considered the possibility of a new way to write music. Ironically, I learned more from these casual conversations than from their formal reports.

The information seemed nonsensical at first, but after reading the reports, I'm not sure what to believe. Despite my initial doubts,

I've decided to let the project continue, something I would have abandoned long ago under normal circumstances.

While the possibility of a hoax remains, the project has taken on a life of its own, seemingly determined to prove its legitimacy. I've never encountered a situation like this. Despite the lack of any digital connection between the Chronologists and Thurston Nogwick, he is about to send them a report that could change everything.

We've downloaded a report from Thurston Nogwick's computer, stored in a word processing program. This report is our primary source of information about the Chronologists, the First Contacts, Stovepipe, and his albums. It represents the first documentation of the artist and his music, but the authenticity of both remains a mystery.

******

Despite my warnings that the project is precarious, my staff remains undeterred. They believe that the evidence of Stovepipe's existence is out there, and that authenticating his albums is more important than the conventional approach of simply acquiring the first and last LP albums and the first CD to define the transition from LP to CD. My staff believes that this transition from LP to CD is as significant as the shift from BC to AD, and that Stovepipe is the pivotal figure bridging this era.

My staff believes that if Stovepipe and his albums exist, they will provide a more comprehensive understanding of the impact of the record album on the Boomer generation than the conventional approach. Defining the artist and his albums will offer a more insightful perspective on this turning point. Ultimately, this unconventional pursuit of Stovepipe and his albums will yield a richer and more valuable body of knowledge.

My staff rarely embraces unconventional methods, which always makes me uneasy. In the past, these approaches have often resulted in disappointing outcomes, where the cost of acquisition outweighed the value of the artifact. However, it's also true that some of the most valuable items in my collection were acquired through these unconventional means.

Based on my current understanding, the project seems to be more about the pursuit of knowledge than the acquisition of valuable artifacts, yet my staff remains committed. They're working late hours without complaint, increasingly convinced that the project is gaining momentum.

We know what message we want to convey to the Chronologists, but we have limited information about them. Essentially, we know they are our competition. At this point, we can only speculate about their identities and motivations based on the information we've gathered.

The Chronologists clearly have a deep understanding of their goals and are determined to achieve them. Our investigation has revealed their seriousness in pursuing their objectives.

We believe the Chronologists are convinced that Stovepipe's albums exist, but they are unsure of his current status. They seem eager to establish that he is deceased. They understand that audiences can transcend death, as evidenced by the continued popularity of many deceased artists, scholars, statesmen, and philosophers. Their strategy is to unveil Stovepipe's identity to the world, gain control of his estate and the copyrights to his albums, and then leverage this newfound knowledge to expand his audience through a series of public pronouncements and revelations.

The Chronologists understand that the estates of deceased celebrities like Elvis Presley, Marilyn Monroe, J.R.R. Tolkien, Jimi Hendrix, and Steve McQueen generate significant revenue. In some years, Elvis and Marilyn's estates have brought in over $50 million. They are attempting to replicate this success with Stovepipe, hoping to elevate his image and launch him into the public consciousness with maximum impact. While unconventional in their approach, the Chronologists are intelligent enough to potentially succeed. They are seeking to control the Stovepipe brand, including his name and likeness. Their motives are primarily economic, and my staff believes their ultimate goal is to establish themselves as a powerful, clandestine financial force.

Our primary sources of information are Thurston Nogwick's interactions with the First Contacts, including those copied on the emails, and the report he is about to send to the Chronologists. We have categorized this data into two types: Report Data and Mail Data. The Report Data suggests that Stovepipe is deceased. However, while tracking all correspondence, we discovered a single individual who has yet to be verified. This person appears only once in the 6,038 documents we have analyzed in the Mail Data. Their only response was a single word: 'awake'.

Even more significant, our documents hint at a 'second coming,' a figure poised to surpass even Elvis in stature. A CD created in 1975 is set for release, marking a defining moment for this individual and a significant turning point. Stovepipe was ahead of his time, with others taking seven years to catch up to his innovations. His albums and influence were instrumental in the transition from LP to CD in 1982, as Stovepipe had already produced a compact disc years before they became mainstream.

Stovepipe has produced and performed on six LP albums and one CD album, pioneering a new direction in music. Document analysis reveals him as a visionary, so far ahead of his time that he remains largely unknown to the public. His influence is evident in the work of other artists, but only a select few have heard his music, and they either keep his influence a secret or claim it as their own. A movement is underway to bring Stovepipe's music to a wider audience, gradually introducing him to the public consciousness.

My staff has conducted a frequency analysis of all the words in the documents, revealing a recurring phrase: 'It's coming.' These two words, 'It' and 'coming,' are the most frequent, appearing first and second in the word distribution. The third most frequent word is 'time.'

The word frequency analysis reveals that all parties communicate using their unique code. It appears that the First Contacts share a unified language among themselves. Interestingly, some frequently used words like 'cat' or 'wig' are employed in unconventional ways, suggesting hidden messages within their seemingly nonsensical exchanges. This cryptic communication style seems designed to mask their true intentions.

Among the 6,038 documents, there is one unidentified individual whose single-word reply hints at their awareness of unfolding events. This elusive figure has remained mysterious thus far. While we are aware of Thurston Nogwick's upcoming release to the Chronologists, it's possible this enigmatic person is also privy to this information.

According to Nogwick's files in the Report Data, the First Contacts assert that Stovepipe is deceased, aligning with the Chronologists' objectives. In the absence of identifying this individual, we speculate that Stovepipe may still be alive. We suspect that this unidentified person could be aiming for a resurrection of sorts.

A critical scenario is unfolding where the Chronologists aim to reveal Stovepipe as deceased but fear the possibility of him being alive upon their announcement. If they discover he is indeed alive, they might resort to extreme measures. The staff has discerned this potential from the word frequency analysis in the Mail Data.

The frequent appearance of certain words suggests a risk that they might manipulate circumstances to align with their announcement in case Stovepipe is alive. Every detail must align perfectly, as they are keen to avoid any chance of a comeback. Their strategy involves leveraging Thurston Nogwick to ensure their plan succeeds.

Given their ambitions, the Chronologists are desperate to avoid being proven wrong. They have meticulously planned a series of announcements designed to cultivate public interest in Stovepipe as a new prophet, generating substantial profits. A living Stovepipe would disrupt their plans, but a deceased Stovepipe could be easily manipulated.

My staff believes the Chronologists are ruthless enough to eliminate any obstacle that threatens their carefully crafted narrative, potentially through Thurston Nogwick or one of his associates. The possibility that this has already happened to others cannot be dismissed.

If the unidentified individual is confirmed to be Stovepipe, we should inform him. While he may be aware of his status as a person of interest, he might not realize the lengths the Chronologists will go to manipulate the situation.

We believe he is aware of the information the First Contacts have shared with the Chronologists and that he feels he has the choice to remain 'dead' or to return. However, the Chronologists will not allow either option. His fate is sealed; he will be eliminated.

This new obligation adds a layer of complexity to our mission of identifying the artist and acquiring his albums, regardless of his current status. We'll address this issue when necessary.

Our research and analysis have led us to conclude that the Chronologists are a well-funded, clandestine organization driven by economic motives, where the ends justify the means.

The Chronologists have inadvertently defined a shared objective for us, which we now intend to pursue. We must not underestimate them; they will be formidable adversaries in this race.

This is the theory, one that I find myself wavering between believing and disbelieving. Perhaps the reason I've allowed the project to continue is because of its hold on my staff. In fact, I'm starting to share their enthusiasm; the project is becoming increasingly captivating for me as well.

While I'm unsure about the validity of the theory, I do know that organizing and verifying the vast amount of information we've gathered based on a nine-word online offer—"Any record albums -

made by Stovepipe - name your price"—is proving to be costly. So far, the theory has only demonstrated that this expense seems inconsequential.

At times, I suspect my staff has overestimated the Chronologists, perhaps chasing a phantom and dragging us along. In my view, the best they can achieve is to establish Stovepipe as a mythical figure, akin to Johnny Appleseed or Paul Bunyan, a legend.

I remain skeptical about the individual who revealed Stovepipe's 'awakening.' I believe the artist and his albums don't exist. I've expressed this view to my staff on multiple occasions, but each time they present a wealth of evidence to the contrary.

Despite my initial skepticism, the document research and analysis presented by my staff has consistently challenged my position. The statistical findings from the document analysis and word distribution strongly suggest that the artist and his albums are real.

This is a crucial turning point. We're on the verge of something significant. The Chronologists, First Contacts (FC), and Thurston Nogwick are convinced that Stovepipe and his albums will surface. This project, along with its key players, has a knack for avoiding closure.

My staff is eager to infiltrate this group of seven key players: Nogwick and his six contacts.

My staff is eager to embark on some investigative trips, but for now, I'm not authorizing any travel. They know this, yet the topic resurfaces at every meeting. It's become a recurring theme, but I have my reasons for withholding approval.

As I've gotten to know my staff and reviewed the background checks on the seven key individuals, I've noticed unsettling similarities between them and the First Contacts. Both groups have the same number of members. Furthermore, the dynamic between Thurston Nogwick and myself mirrors the relationship between the collector and those working for the Chronologists—a one-to-one correspondence. This parity makes me uneasy. I prefer a more significant advantage, ideally a three-to-one ratio.

One of the seven individuals' backgrounds struck me as eerily familiar, a mirror image of someone on my staff, including myself. I spend a great deal of time with my team, but my knowledge of the First Contacts comes solely from the reports. What I've read about them is unusual, and it's causing me to question my perception of my own staff. Perhaps they are not as ordinary as I've always believed, and perhaps I am changing as well. Everything about this project seems to be out of the ordinary.

The truth is, we're all captivated by the nine-word offer. Typically, I set a budget limit for artifacts on every project, but with Stovepipe and his albums, no one has even considered it. We're all consumed by the singular goal of establishing the artist's authenticity. It's become a contest—the staff against the First Contacts, the collector against the Chronologists.

******

Our theory is evolving based on the information we've gathered through document surveillance and analysis of both Report Data and Mail Data. We anticipate that Thurston Nogwick will soon forward his Word files to the Chronologists, which will provide us with new avenues to explore. We hope that this event will reveal the missing pieces of the puzzle.

The Nogwick Files (Report Data) contain verbatim transcripts from six individuals who possess a wealth of information about the artist and his albums, exceeding fifty thousand words. Email tracking has added another one hundred thousand words, providing us with enough material to write a book about the artist.

Nogwick hired professionals to interview and record the First Contacts' knowledge, creating a system that only requires him to press "send" to the designated address. Currently, aside from our computers, Nogwick's computer is the sole repository of the complete files. However, the computers, files, and the six individuals involved in the interview and recording process have vanished.

He may have found people who wanted to disappear. On the other hand, they may have become people who needed to disappear once the information was gathered. Either way, we've lost contact with them; this is the first time some targets have dropped off our radar. It's a concern, but this is a mystery that, for now, can wait. What is important now is what the FC says about the artist and his albums.

These facts hold our interest concerning the six individuals who make up the First Contacts. All are male; however, there are a number of females copied in their e-mails. All were born in Ohio between 1948 and 1953. All are white, and at the time they were interviewed, the age range of the six FCs was fifty- nine to sixty-four.

In their accounts, the earliest year referenced is 1968; the latest year is 1973. During this five-year period, their age range would've been fifteen to twenty in 1968 and twenty to twenty-five in 1973. At these ages, within this five-year interval, each recalls all the events that happened in one day, thirty-four to thirty-nine years ago, the event Stovepipe.

All six of the FC have a high school diploma; four went onto college; two have degrees. All served in the armed forces; two were drafted into the army, two enlisted in the Air Force, one enlisted in the Marines, and one enlisted in the Navy. The enlistments in the Marines and Navy were alternatives offered by the court.

Three are married, three divorced, and five have children. Four are above the median income line for Ohio; two are below the line. All know each other; all have mentioned the Chronologists in their transcripts.

None are musicians. None know of Thurston Nogwick, or believe the person who conducted their interview is Nogwick. None would be able to identify him.

All have had a firsthand, one-on-one encounter with Stovepipe. All were paid for the interview; this is when they became aware of the Chronologists. All view them with suspicion, but it's not enough to stop them from taking payment for what they know. All replied to the nine-word offer with information and items they had related to the albums that might be for sale. They said enough to get Nogwick's attention. So far, not one item has been sold, only information.

We've learned from e-mails all declined an interview, until each was hit with some financial crisis, painting them into a corner where the interview looked good. On one hand, they feel like some python has coiled around them, squeezing them for information. Thurston Nogwick and the Chronologists make them uncomfortable, but on the other hand, pay them well for what they say they know.

Through our analysis, it is becoming apparent the First Contacts would be the model of what the Chronologists want to develop in the public. The impact Stovepipe has on them is the same impact they want to reproduce on a certain percentage of the public. From the tele-evangelists, they know there are a percentage of vulnerable people out there who will buy into anything if it's presented in a saving format.

Everyone is interested in a second coming. The FC is providing the information necessary for the development of how this could be accomplished. The FC will be set up as the disciples of the 'First Believers' in the evolution of the awareness of Stovepipe. Stovepipe will become the prophet they follow. When this evolution runs its course, the dollars will come from these First Believers.

All observations point to Stovepipe as a charismatic, ritualistic individual. He's known to wear a patch over one eye; no one can agree which eye. At times, it's a black patch; at other times, it's a black patch with a musical note on it. It's believed he has the use of both eyes but chooses to use one. He dresses in three colors, black, white, and gray, the way he views the world. He wants to appear like some character from a black-and-white movie in a world of color, purposely out of place.

When the patch moves from one eye to the other or one color of his clothing begins to dominate the other two, he ritualistically signals a change in direction. All those recording artists fortunate enough to have caught the changes have become great. All the contacts comment on the rituals behind the patch and the attire. The change that came from Stovepipe each contact caught first hand.

Also mentioned is the fact he was a child prodigy; no note, no voice, no instrument was beyond him; he could read music before he could talk. There is a reference that as he got older, common musical notation didn't provide what is necessary to capture his work, so he developed his own musical notation. A notation developed to bring out the best sound of any instrument and voice. There are said to be some albums that introduce this best sound through the new notation.

This is only part of the background. The other part is he has an intuitive gift for understanding the technology behind and operating any piece of equipment that was and is used in a recording studio to its full potential. It's been said the bedrock of all the innovations that took place in the recording industry is found in the work he produced between 1968 and 1978, the six vinyl LPs and one plastic CD. He dropped off the radar around 1982. He's been dead or dormant for over thirty years.

The analysis points to Marietta, Ohio, as Stovepipe's birthplace. He was born late 1952, early 1953. This location and time range have the highest probability from our research. However, we are yet to establish the true origin of location and time as fact.

The staff informs me this is because there are several regions, not only in Ohio but also the country, claiming Stovepipe. Our frequency distributions point to the existence of a very small knowledgeable subculture in each quadrant of the country: Northeast, Southeast, Northwest, and Southwest, providing conflicting information as to location and time. Marrietta—1952, 1953—is our best statistical guess.

A straight line is drawn on the map from one point to the other. Marietta is at one end, Cleveland at the other. The direction of the history moves northeast from Marietta to Cleveland over a thirty-year period starting in 1952 and ending in 1982 to take in all possible events. The mentioned highways and interstates exits to the small towns and cities leading to Cleveland gather around this line during this period. The number of places mentioned varies from this line by no more than fifty miles; some are right on the line.

We know the most about the northeastern subculture. All the information on the subcultures from the other three regions comes from persons copied in and responding to the situation the First Contacts of the northeast subculture find themselves in.

All four regional subcultures share the age range of the five-year period starting in 1968 through 1973. It's felt like all regions came in contact with Stovepipe during this period. Stovepipe and the First Contacts are all in the same age range. They speak of Stovepipe as the first person close to their age who was light years beyond them, beyond anyone they ever ran into, then and now.

The northeast subculture has informed the other regions of the Chronologists. All regions speculate as to their motives. If it weren't for the money, all regions would break contact.

The northeast subculture was the only region to respond to the nine-word offer, and from the documents, their response occurred more by accident than design. The nine-word offer seems to have jarred a subconscious part of their mind. Once it surfaced, they talked of how they couldn't stop themselves from responding.

What is fascinating is each of the six First Contacts responded to the offer independently of each other, and each had something to say. It's only after their contact with Nogwick that they become aware of what each had done. There is a short period of e-mails where all have asked each other, "You know Thurston Nogwick?"

The offer mobilized the FC to respond about some artifacts they hold from their past. Each First Contact tells of being on the ground floor of an album Stovepipe made. More than one album is mentioned by them. This is how we know the titles of the six LPs he made between 1968 and 1973.

It's said he produced five hundred copies of each. Only three thousand vinyl LP albums were made. If all still exist, it would have a distribution, at this time, of one album per one hundred thousand people (man, woman, and child). We know this is probably not the case, given the timeframe. If they exist, the distribution is probably closer to one per half million. They're scarce for the impact they're said to have.

The chronology of the albums is always a debate among the First Contacts. The debate centers around which albums are pre-'Beaufort' and which are Beaufort. The documents analyzed point to the new musical notation created by Stovepipe is based on the Beaufort wind scales. In that, music puts motion to sound. This motion is very similar to the wind.

These Beaufort albums are said to have had the most influence over the great artists of our time. However, it's pointed out by the FC that as great as these artists are and were, these artists can only imitate the Beaufort sound. They're trying to play Beaufort, but only Stovepipe has accomplished this. All point out that if you heard Beaufort, you'd know the difference, and you'd be changed.

When Beaufort actually arrived during this five-year period can't be agreed upon by the FC. Pre-Bufford albums are even rarer; each tries to explain if the album they were associated with is one or the other. All regional subcultures are unclear on the Beaufort chronology. For now, all that is known is it surfaced between 1968 and 1973.

All the First Contacts refer to themselves by a nickname given to them by Stovepipe. We have their real names, but in the transcripts, they go by a name ordained by Stovepipe. For the time being, their true identity will remain confidential. The initial documentation will use their ordained names. We've been counseled on privacy issues. Their true identity will come if and when these issues are no longer a concern in the final phase of documentation.

The chronology revealed in the Nogwick files starts out with 'Spoon' giving the oral history of the *Save Your Strength* album. This is followed by 'Noose,' who has the history of the *Bagpipes and Bongo's* album. There's *Atomic Peanut,* according to 'Motor,' *Radio Ventriloquist,* presented by 'Dart,' *Sticks to Bricks* told by 'Boat' and *Good Wood* by 'Book.' These are the six vinyl LPs: the first chronology, Beaufort, and pre-Beaufort. The Nogwick files are the oral history of the Stovepipe vinyl period and reside in our Report Data.

All information on the compact disc resides in our Mail Data. We are trying to make the connection from one email, where the writer claims to be Stovepipe, to our unidentified person. However, so far, the connection can't be made, verified, or proven. It looks like there should be a fit, an alignment, but there isn't.

We are also yet to get his identity and he plays the role of either imposter or informer. There have been Stovepipe impersonators in the past. Then again, he could be presenting the script written by the one who is "awake." We don't know.

We've also included a compilation of this email in additionto the oral history of the Nogwick files. We know the seventh album is called by two names, *Pipe Reloaded* or *Bloodstream* and is a CD.

Whether this is the true chronology is unknown, but these are the seven albums of Stovepipe. We seem to be under the spell of the history behind the artist and the albums.

******

It has been nine months since we first came across the nine-word offer on the net. We have a ton of information but no identification or artifacts. According to my staff, both are just around the corner.

I'll give them one more quarter to come up with something concrete. Thurston Nogwick is yet to send his report to the Chronologists. The staff believes once this occurs, a quick solution will be at hand.

No one can adequately explain why this hasn't happened yet— other than the unspoken feeling we may be, for the first time, on someone else's radar. The staff thinks I'm unaware oftheir concern this might be happening. We're no closer to the Chronologists, our unidentified person, or the artifacts. All we know is what is supposed to exist. To go forward, something has to surface as a fact.

Something other than a record jacket, sales slip, record shard, album in the unknown safety deposit box, the album in a coffin, and reels of magnetic tape, all of which the First Contacts claim to have as proof of the existence of *their* album.

Initially, the FC put these items up for sale in their responseto the nine-word offer. The staff feels they can authenticate these items. These items are hardly evidence as all can be counterfeit. I've made the staff aware. The standard is an identified artist and playable album, end of subject, subjectclosed.

I'll open up the offense in the last quarter; maybe authorizesome trips to the regions. I'll put three on the northeastern subculture and three on the other regional subcultures. Of the three I send northeast, two will be on Book and one on the other five. Book has the highest probability for results.

But I won't give more time. To date, audits covering salary, benefits, hardware, software, research, and communications put project expenditures a little over $750,000. So far, all end costs; just tracking down the seven albums is around $107,000per album. I'm willing to go twice the amount per album in thelast quarter.

I've also made the staff aware of a legal reserve I've set aside for the invasion of privacy issues that may come up from our approach. They're covered. I have created a bonus system for results. The budget for the last quarter will equal theexpenditures of the first three quarters. My impatience will open up the purse, but it won't stay open beyond the last quarter.

It's been decided to put out what we know. The staff

believes as we go into the last quarter, opening the artist and albums to a wider public could improve our probabilities of establishing the artist and obtaining the albums. With time running out, it's felt a wider net has to be thrown to gather it all in. Even though the possibility exists, we may be playing into the hands of the Chronologists doing their work.

On the other hand, it's come down to a war of documentation. From the very beginning, I've been upfront about the approach we've taken—our capabilities and the legal issues we're prepared to face. The Chronologist will have to prove we stole their thunder; we will be the first to document what is known about the artist and albums.

Sooner or later, if what's said to be out there exists, it will show up in their or our crosshairs. No one has lost the scent. It's a question of who can get into range of the objective first.

What is presented in the Nogwick Files and compilation file, covering the seven albums, defies common sense and logic, as if both don't matter in what is told. Yet, at the same time, what is told has all the characteristics of a strange reality. I want—we want—to know the artist, hear the albums.

After reading these transcripts, if you know the artist or have one or all of the albums, we need to talk: 4563boomer.com

Prologue to the Vinyl Records

All information on the vinyl records resides in our Record Data. The narrative of six vinyl record albums produced by Stovepipe has been captured from Thurston Nogwick's Word files. The data from these files is linear, sequential, and fairly stable. This stability should not be confused with reliability. However, there are certain patterns that repeat themselves and become predictable in the sequence of events.

From the Record Data covering these albums, we're confident Stovepipe appeared towards the end of the LP to CD era (1948 - 1982), his influence surfacing in 1968 and continuing through 1982, when he disappeared from sight, presumed dead. It appears during the thirty-four-year period from LP to CD; he occupied fourteen years of the interval, hisactivity during this time covering forty percent of the period.

The First Contacts share the common thread of interaction;each has given their full account of the impact of running intoStovepipe and catching his tunes. There's a pattern in the data where it's found these meetings were never planned. All ran into Stovepipe by accident. The data gives the appearance these meetings were random events, but at the same time, there are indicators in some of the data that seem to point that theymay have been planned for a reason.

The reason is unclear or can't be adequately explained. Record Data presents six accounts in a sequence, starting with Spoon and ending with Book. Whether this is the order the six FCs were interviewed or whether Thurston Nogwick set this chronology is yet to be determined. We lean toward Nogwick in that they are sequenced by the first and last year mentioned(1968 to 1973).

Point being the chronology is always debated. The FC interviews bring to the surface the sequence of these albums seems to be of major importance to the Chronologists.

Finally, Stovepipe is spoken of in more than one voice, real and imagined. If the six accounts on the albums offer anything, it's the decision to be made between the two. We're left in a position where our Record Data points that all of the events could have happened but can't directly prove they did. We're left with what is said to exist.

Album 1: Save Your Strength (According to Spoon)

He probably figured it out sliding down the birth canal – *better save your strength*. He had the big gig down from the beginning and upfront. And at the point where he knew nothing about life on the outside, boom! Just inches before he made thebig slide, he put it all together on the inside.

Life, the big gig – don't know when it's going to start, don'tknow when it's going to end. No one knows how long the showis going to run. Only get so many beats on stage, the trick is toput each lick to good use before it's over; lot of songs in the big gig, some happy, some sad, some good, some bad.

He took these thoughts, folded them neatly together, and stuck them in the pockets of his subconscious. An insidereference for his travels on an outside sliding scale of good and bad. Decided he wanted the weight to come down on the side of good, and did it all on the inside, on his slide outside.

And once he made the big slide, his life became a scenic mystery of what was and wasn't Stovepipe. He knew light anddark, spirit and flesh. He had the inside blessing and the outside curse. Only ten people really knew him, but those ten knew tenwho knew ten so that by the time the big gig was over and his unknown interval became known to everyone but him, the biography was the full Winston—never had so many cats wigged so much to get so little. In fact, when it came to the Pipe, the more you caught, the more you dropped. He was beyond ordinary radar.

******

Stovepipe put it down, and old Spoon here picked it up one afternoon in 1968. For the time being, I'm going to put a cat onyou who cleared up human nature for me. Human nature moves in two gears: conscious and subconscious, what we see and what we dream. At times, human nature finds it hard to separate the real from the imagined. That it's in our nature to combine the two and call it history. Human nature orbits around change and can be influenced in many ways. One way is 'tunes' (music). Everyone has a tune running through their head. This is our nature, and there are good and bad tunes. There's a story behind *Save Your Strength*.

It was shortly after we'd made it back to the "world." We weren't together over there. It was just something we had in common. We were in Ohio, somewhere near Delaware, the geographic center of the state, heading northeast. That afternoon, a non-stop rap began that at one point was stall-to- stall in the men's room at the Truck Stop Supreme off I-71, shortly after pounding down two open-face pork sandwiches covered in gravy and grease. Once everything got started, nothing could stop it. The whole afternoon and night was like living a dream to where one couldn't tell what gear they were in, conscious or subconscious. Can't put together exactly why we were traveling 71 or how we got together, but somehow, it all started in Athens. And Athens is just as much a blur now as it was back then. I remember I wanted a ride to Columbus. Ran into Pipe, and it was on the way. Pipe was heading to Cleveland with a stop in Akron. "The shotgun seat is yours," he told me after saying goodbye to some knockout chick.

All that comes back is how we rode the Comet through Nelsonville, Logan, Lancaster, past Columbus, on up to Delaware, Ashland, and then Akron. Just off my original destination by three towns. On a warm, clear autumn day, that told me, "Just keep going with it." The attitude worked a little too well. I was sitting in

Delaware when I realized we alreadycruised through Columbus.

We cruised over land in a red and white 63 Comet, all cylinders sliding over the hills and through the woods, and after a while, began to look for a place to eat. Found a place around Delaware, the Truck Stop Supreme, the only stop we made.

It was quite a ride. The woods on both sides of the road were showing off their blended colors of yellow, orange, and red. The rolling fields of the farms in shades of green were turning to shades of brown. Ohio always shows its colors before the black, white, and gray of winter.

In Ohio, maybe 280 people per square mile, and it seemed everyone within a square mile of the truck stop was there that day. It was crowded and loud, bordering on chaos. It was a place and a moment that held all sexes, ages, races, outfits, attitudes, and natures a square mile of Ohio can produce – goodand bad.

The town people, those from the farm, and those on the road were all there. The inside of the place was as colorful as the outside. It was lively. Everyone was busy. They placated theircustomers with coffee. And at the time, we were in touch withour excesses and probably knocked back ten cups of coffee anda pack of smokes as if we were the only ones there experiencing leisure in an atmosphere of chaos.

Stovepipe had that wiry build and the look of someone whowas just coming down with something or just getting over something. There are few times I feel better looking than whoI'm with, and this was one of them. The waitress was cute. Shecould write an order without looking at her pad; she never tookher eyes off Pipe, and I never took my eyes off her. Seemed tome all the eye contact was backwards. I was puzzled.

In short, my long, thick hair, cool Fu Manchu, and good build were all trumped by Pipe's charisma. Knowing when to talk, when to pause; he spoke more with his eyes than his mouth. I just looked the part, but Pipe *was* the part. He was magnetic; knew all the angles.

When the plates finally made the table, that's when it started, and the personal history of the Stovepipe began to unwind like a tightly coiled spring with plenty behind it that, when decompressed, moves fast and turns out to be twice the size. And at that moment, the chaotic atmosphere surrounding us turned calm and no louder than a library. It all started at the Truck Stop Supreme around Delaware. The time and place of the album surfaced like an atomic sub off the coastline of my mind.

The only place we stopped still crosses my mind to this day. I've done a lot of truck stops, but none like the Supreme. Over the years, I've wanted to go back, but something always comes up. Wonder if I could even find it. It's probably changed hands a bunch of times or been torn down. It was a long time ago, but one of these days.

******

In a way, I go back to the Supreme all the time. I can still see Pipe gazing at the big rigs crammed on the asphalt when he brought up the calling hours of a buddy cat that pulled the trigger on himself, who ended his own gig, a cat that was found with not one, but two guns, one for each hand, in case one didn't work. "There was a bullet in his head and one in the floor. Took that steel dick in his mouth and blew off the back of his head. It was war ugly," Pipe told me. I didn't have a problem getting the picture and thought to myself it wasn't the first time I'd heard something like this. It wasn't uncommon, but the 'uncommon' was on its way.

Pipe was close enough with the cat in the box to show up, but that was about it. "This cat ended his own gig. You don't get to do that. Cheated his audience. Friends," Pipe footnoted. I had never heard of the cat in the box, but he had a lot of influence on those who showed up. Pipe mentioned enough really big names to make me wish I'd made the scene. The Cat in the Box brought a lot of big names out of the woodwork. Hewas important enough to have Pipe there.

Where you'd expect some talk about the names mentioned, the Pipe went on a never-ending, fifteen-minute rap about the chair he was sitting in during the calling hours, right down to the wing backs and the leather that covered them, and if he'd had footstool, he'd be coming up with more of what he was putting down.

He admitted to being overpowered by the chair. And I learned as he rapped on that everyday objects—cars, chairs, toasters, vacuum cleaners, coffee makers, drinking fountains—you name it, could at times produce a stream of consciousnessfrom the Pipe that plants, animals, or people couldn't.

Pipe was inorganic. This is important. See, most of the recognition comes from his tunes, but Pipe was also very technical. What he put out it was explosive. We wouldn't be catching his tunes if he didn't have a delivery system. There wasn't a speaker, amp, microphone, tape, or control panel; he didn't know inside out, blindfolded. Stovepipe could pluck notes out of the air, hook them up with the perfect lyrics punctuated by the right voice, then cut them on the highest quality vinyl. He related better to machines than people, plants, and animals. In fact, nature seemed to scare him.

Getting back to the cat in the box, down the line, I've caught some of the ordinary cats that made the room that day, and one of the first things they'd tell you is the Stovepipe was there for sure, and for obvious reasons that was a big deal. They say he stayed the full two hours and said little to those around him. His mind wasn't on the Cat in the Box. As far as the Pipe was concerned, that Cat was just that: the Cat in the Box and nothing more.

All the idols of the time were there for this cat. The ordinary cats knew the crowd but, like me, never heard of Cat in the Box. He was as unknown to them as the crowd was known to them. The ordinary cats tagged along to this event. Pipe hardly paid anyone any mind. The ordinary cats say Pipe got up once to catch a smoke and then went back to the chair that every big- name cat in the crowded room knew better than to take during his absence. They say his mind was elsewhere – on all the cats, man, woman, and child that ever sat in the chair. It's when he returned to the chair that he went into his vision.

Some say the patch was on his right eye that day; others say it was over the left, adding to the myth that the Stovepipe only had one eye. But in either case, it was before he put the musical note on the patch and formed the band *Stovepipe and the Big Notes*. Every once in a while, a band shows up with a cat wearing a patch; it's a sign they know or heard about the Pipe. For sure, you don't see it often, but they're out there, and the bands are pretty tight. The patch is an underground thing I'm not going to get into now. What's important is everything Pipe told me about the calling hours and the rites that took place, matched up with everything the ordinary cats told me. Stovepipe had validity.

I can see Pipe continually sliding a pack of matches between the thumb and forefinger of his right hand while at the same time rearranging the napkin holder and the salt and pepper shakers with his left, talking nonstop at the Supreme. It wasn't hard to figure out what put the fuel behind his words; the speed was in a special place in his right boot under the table that was always too easy to get to. One of those outside curses mentioned earlier. A lot of things that are bad, Pipe thought, were good.

That day at the Supreme, he rapped on about the funeral parlor where it all took place. The Aces and Eights Funeral Home, whose clientele was made up of high-end bikers, radicals, and anyone else on the edge, the "Home" as it's known only to certain subcultures. It operated paperless: no license, no records, no phone, an underground funeral home, literally and figuratively. No, really. It once was a large fallout shelter on some long-forgotten estate that only a small minority knew about. They put some cash together and bought the place. Later that day, he showed me where it was when I showed him my doubt that such a place existed outside his head. It was on the way. It's still the best side trip I've ever taken to this day.

In an odd way, the chair was starting to make sense against this backdrop. He pointed out we weren't far from the home. It was located nearby, and he dialed up the vision he had in the chair there like an old girlfriend. Now, I caught most of what he had about this, but not all of it. My mind was still on the rites he described they conducted before he went into his vision.

The rites for the cat in the box to this day are still a stretch, but if the place existed, why wouldn't they've taken place - the releasing of flies, along with the placing of the leeches? The flies released from a packed quart jar of rotting meat, enough to keep you continually swatting at them, symbolizing how bothersome life can be. The leeches taken from some large soup bowl, placed on the forehead to symbolize how in the end, you're sucked dry.

After clearing the flies and removing the leeches, the filling of the bowls, lines on the mirror, needles and the popping of the caps, to get high enough to forget what is waiting down the road. It's not what I would want, but to a certain clientele that try to create heaven on earth by living the moment by what they take, it seems to work. Who knows? I was lost in these rites for a while, thinking a funeral home would be one of the last places I'd want to run into flies and leeches to get high.

I picked him up at the point where he was talking about what he saw while sitting in the mystical chair. He saw a man and woman come together. They were dwarfs sitting on a Greyhound coming out of Toledo in the early 1940s, heading to Akron to work on the Corsairs being built there, two midgets getting into the war effort— War Midgets.

As smoke poured from his nose and mouth, he accented the scene with an afterthought—"All war efforts everywhere and at any time should be on a midget level."—and ended with a sigh. This, in turn, brought on never-ending rap on war, to the point where one couldn't put together if the Pipe was for it or against it, just that he'd been in one, and that was enough. I knew what he was saying. And, yeah, he touched upon the Mounties who'd captured him in Canada and sent him back, but then, as we all know, the Pipe had to be in a really rare mood to rap about his days with the

Mounties. For the time being, the two midgets he left me with on the bus heading to Akron was enough to trump the Mounties.

Once I got him back on track, Pipe bellowed, "Ordinary dwarfs! Not by a long shot! They were short on the outside but long on the inside. They were beyond being dwarfs, midgets, little people, whatever you call them. They knew who they were and didn't have a problem with it. They worked on the Corsairs for a little while, but in the forties, it seemed the only successful fields for midgets were either in the circus or in wrestling. The two opened it up when they formed an all- midget band known for great instrumental solos that were always too short."

The Stovepipe was in full flow after visiting his right boot. And as he talked, I ate, and when he ate, I just sat there trying to put it all together. Three-quarters of an hour to put down two open-faced pork sandwiches, where the last bite didn't taste anything like the first, as the Pipe rolled on.

Somewhere in the past, these two dwarfs seemed to be tied directly to Stovepipe's complete command and understanding of music. Then the Pipe put on me, "Written music showed up between seven to eight hundred years before Christ. Amos, Hosea, and Isaiah were the main cats then. Rome was the maintown, and if you made it anywhere, you made it by chariot. That's when they started putting it down. Yeah, they always told me, tunes are the older brother of the Naz, the Naz and tunes make the world spin, my music comes from the little people."

And from what he was putting down, I drew my firstconclusion that if you ever ran into Howlin' Wolf, T-Bone Walker, Lead Belly, Hank Williams, Bob Wills and his Texas Playboys, or anyone like them, the first question you might be asking all, is if they ever knew any dwarfs from Akron. Turns out only Pipe knew them.

Pipe covered his food with pepper until you couldn't see it and kept it up about the dwarfs, not once ever mentioning any names. And if the Pipe ever had a gift it was taking people in. He had me to the point with the two midgets that I wound up naming them, came up with Vern and Ida out of nowhere. For some reason, my mind pulled them out of thin air.

Found myself saying their names out loud; found Pipe nodding, "Right, Vern and Ida." At the time, I never realized he skillfully set them up in my head. After the setup, every word he dropped from there on fell right into place. The Pipe was nimble. Looking back, the first ten cats I told about Stovepipe know a completely different Stovepipe than the last ten cats; the last bite doesn't taste anything like the first.

But the Pipe had me back then. And tumbling back to that truck stop, I can catch the cat clear as a bell, a big bell. The words and motion in perfect pitch and rhythm like the tunes he was known to put out, and that's why any of the really big cats in tunes, who are and were real, know or knew about Stovepipe – one way or the other, depending on what ten cats they talked to.

With Vern and Ida living in my head, the lineage of how the Pipe came to be sitting across from me had more begets than some chapters in the *Old Testament,* winding and tangling to being the illegitimate son of either Boxcar Willie or Lord Buckley, the woman who carried him never mentioned. The Pipe let me draw a second conclusion that the musical dwarfs, Vern and Ida, raised him

- taking me years to second-guess this second conclusion with the fact that Vern and Ida never reallyexisted beyond our conversation at the Truck Stop Supreme.

But they're in all conversations on Pipe. And in the end, comes from some mystical chair in some bizarre funeral parlor located near the center of Ohio.

******

As that day wore on, Stovepipe's comfort with me grew, confusing my silence as acceptance. There were no two ways about it; he had my attention, but the silence was brought on by my inability to form and ask all the questions I had runningthrough my mind. He was always two or three steps ahead of me, and I made him go over again and again the things I didn't catch first time around. This is when he started calling me 'Spoon.' "Have to spoon-feed you everything."

It was a real honor to be taken into the Pipe's confidence when he unloaded a huge family secret on me. Seems his great- grandfather was the cat that put Stonewall Jackson on the wrong side of the sod six weeks before Gettysburg. As soon asit came out, Pipe wanted to back away from it and move on, but there was no way I was going to let it pass, and my confidence began to expand, and I crowded him on it.

But Pipe took it back to square one. Pointing out, "The Civil War, a mainstay civil drag, according to Lord Buckley, where a lot of cats blew a lot of bad jazz and laid it down and left it there, was the hat trick of issues that could only be resolved by popping one another."

Without hesitation, he went into what was behind the huge

misunderstanding. "Was the cash hauled in going to come from the factory or the farm? What kind of labor are we going to have, paid or slave? Who was going to be calling the shots, the cats downtown or the cats on the farm?" Then he put down that this major hassle, in reality, wasn't about people, it was about cash and who was going to control it, rights coming from the states or the Feds. I'd taken enough American history the previous quarter to put on Pipe, "Here, I thought it was about slavery, you know - Article 1, Section 9, paragraph 4, the South stitched onto our Constitution to make it theirs, check it out."

The speed was kicking in. Pipe leaned back and exhaled a huge cloud of yellowish-white smoke that covered his words. "Dig! Those cats back then had a lot buzzing under their caps. Some of them got pretty stiff about the issues, both sides up and down." He then surprised me when he added, "You know, those 'one ninety-four cats.' came to scrap." Right before I was about to ask, it came to me that the 'one ninety-four' referenced the article, section, and paragraph I had mentioned from the Confederate Constitution, Pipe had picked up on it, and it made me feel good. He continued, "From Bull Run to Appomattox, 2.2 million of them rolling in and out of each other's backyard, to the point that when it finally did grind down, 640 K wound up in the wrong yard at the wrong time, and on the wrong side of the sod at the time the biggest percentage loss of population due to war the land had ever seen. The issues just became too big to rap about; took more than one hassle site to come up with something new."

I wanted to apply the brakes to the Pipe, wanted to get back to the cat that took Stonewall out six weeks before Gettysburg. Not that what he was putting down wasn't interesting, but being a northern boy from Ohio and a victim of my own human nature, I wanted the Pipe to tell me his great-grandfather was an Ohio boy. For all I knew at the time, Stovepipe was an Ohio boy. Now I'm here to tell you, ask any ten cats, and you'll get ten different states, north and south, east and west that claim him, but if his great grandfather was an Ohio boy, why the family secret? If he was an Ohio boy, he wouldn't back away from taking Stonewall out; who'd want keep that a secret?

I tuned the Pipe out for a while as I wrestled with the question and was just getting ready to ask him point blank about gramps, but when I tuned him back in, I picked him up where he was comparing William Tecumseh Sherman to Stonewall and again got lost in his rap.

Caught him just as he was getting into Sherm's middle name, pointing out that it was the name of a great Indian chief, and up north where Sherm came from, people for a long time did nothing but fight with the Indians. Tecumseh fought hard enough to get the respect of the Shermans, his middle name unusual for the time. It was a little too ironic that his middle name gave some insight into what kind of cat he might be. And as it turned out, Sherm was all that was advertised. "He'd make Georgia howl." It seemed the Pipe dug him, and Sherm was an Ohio boy, but then again, I've been around enough to know that if you ask any ten cats from the South, their big hearts will tell you Pipe was a Stonewall cat for sure. They have their story.

According to the Pipe, Sherm and Stonewall were just two characters caught up in the Hegelian model of thesis, antithesis, and synthesis. He then put a lot of wind behind what he was talking about. "See, it only goes from cool to not cool, to new cool, 'new cool,' a mixture of the first two. For example, the farms cool, no, the city is cool - then boom! The suburbs."

He didn't stop there. "Back then, it was all urban or rural. If you were in town and want a new scene, your only move is the farm, and vice versa. They're two different camps, but that's cool, one can't make without the other, they're even. Asfar as where you are, it's one of two paces on the board. You're either in town or on the farm, and if you're in between, you're a refugee. We've both caught what I'm talking about." I lit a smoke and nodded.

It was beginning to flow, but I wanted to apply the brakes as Pipe core dumped like a computer and returned to Stonewall and Gramps. Just couldn't get it done because, as I thought about it, Pipe was right—you want to change the scene back then, and there you only have two moves, urban or rural. So I continued to move over the hills and bends of his mind,catching the scenery, unable to stop where I wanted.

It was starting to get heavy, and Stovepipe could play it to the point that what you wanted to find out would be the last thing you'd get from him. That is what you thought you were getting closer to. You were actually getting farther from it. I had a chance to put on the brakes when we signaled for more coffee, but he had me to where I wanted to go wherever he wasgoing.

We stayed with Sherm and Stonewall - Pipe contrasting their philosophies: "See, with Sherm it was all: take, make, and think. *Take* and *make* this gig so nasty that every cat is going to *think* twice about going off to Hasselville." He then lit a smoke and continued, "With Stonewall, it was all: hold, change, and take. *Hold* on to everything, don't try to *change* a thing, and for real, don't try to *take* anything." Wound it up ina cloud of smoke. "You know what it's going to rain when two fronts like this bang into each other?"

It was kind of starting to come together; we were at least getting back to Stonewall and maybe his great-grandfather. Butthat was just wishful thinking. We were going to go beyond hisgreat-grandfather and Stonewall and on into how the South actually won the war.

This was about the time I caught Stovepipe's reflection in the huge window that gave the view of the parking lot. The waythe light hit the dark pavement and the clear glass, the way it bounced around, it produced an image of him on the glass in black and white with shades of gray. He became a black and white movie as he rapped on about how the South won the war.I was really never looking at him, but at his reflection, the reflection providing far more impact on what was unfolding aswe went back in time.

I watched his reflection as he reached inside his coat and produced a fine leather billfold that perfectly fit the period of time being talked about. Tooled leather with Old Glory and theStars and Bars tattooed on it. He opened it and dropped the very old photos of two young men on the table. I turned from the reflection and looked at them for a while, and as I reached for a smoke, I turned back to his reflection, unable to do anythingelse.

From the reflection, Pipe began to lean forward onto the table, coyly lifting the patch over his right eye to find a pack ofmatches hiding behind an overfilled ashtray. Then he asked, "You know Albert Woolson - how about John Salling?" I thought for a moment and then answered his reflection. "No idea." Pipe paused and then shot back, "Well, they're both on the table."

Turned out the first photo was of Albert Woolson, the last Union soldier to die at the age of 109 on August 2, 1956. Turned out the second photo was of John Salling, the last Confederate soldier to die at the age of 112 on March 16, 1958. I got caught up in the ages and dates, realizing I was no younger than eight and no older than ten when both died. I would've guessed the two events happening way before I was born.

Pipe formulated the following, "What you do is subtract their ages, Woolson's from Salling's, then the years apart from when each died, and add the answers together." It was right after he lit his smoke that he put on me, "South doesn't need torise again, they won by five – make it six; the cat from the South was born a year before the cat from the North... The whole contest was pretty close – but yeah, the South by six."

I never forgot the facts behind that math, and from that point, I lost control of ever getting back to Stonewall Jackson and Pipe's great-grandfather. And if any ten cats lay on you, that the Pipe was related to not one, but both of the last cats, both sides, that made the Civil War, they probably got it from me. Yeah, they'd probably tell you they got it from "Spoon," to make it real, back in the day when I was kind of a junior varsity Stovepipe. But the fact is, I really don't know, but thinkthey all could be related.

The Pipe could rap on about these two boys like they were family, right down to their shoe size. And by the time he got tohow each caught all "Three Fires," he had me wrapped up tighter than a golf ball. I turned from the reflection in the window and looked right at him, pulled a smoke from my shirt pocket, and asked, "What three fires? What are you talking about?" -ready to call him on any little goof up. After a quick review of the cat in the box, the mystical chair, these two boys,which I seemed to be accepting with little questioning, Idecided to become a little more skeptical. But try as I may, thisdidn't work.

My question was what he was waiting for. A signal I was now off the trail of his great-grandfather. The one I wanted to take. We were on a new trail, the one he wanted to take. It wasat this point that Albert Woolson and John Salling became "Uncle Albert" and "Uncle John." Like the explanation of his lineage, Pipe was able to wind and tangle the two down to theconvoluted fact that one of the *Beatles* knew *Uncle Albert, whocouldn't go to sea.* And you didn't really have to guess how Little Richard came up with *Uncle John back in the alley.* Explaining their relationship to him.

And somewhere along the line, the Pipe must have visited that right boot under the table, and how he pulled it off, I don'tknow because he was in front of me the whole time. But then again, his patch was probably over his left eye when we took off from the Supreme. He was getting that cagy. Seems when we went in, it was over the right. Like his lineage, you just couldn't know for sure.

******

The Pipe began explaining the Three Fires after we ordered desert. "See, first we started borrowing fire from nature, 'Original Fire,' had to wait for the lightning strike. Couple of hundred years later, or whatever, started rubbing sticks (fire byfriction), then up the road striking flint and steel (fire by percussion), then matches (fire by chemicals), All variations ofOriginal fire. When Uncle Albert and Uncle John made the scene, that's where we were at, chemicals." He continued, "And if you wanted to do something good or bad with fire, allyou really had were matches to get things rolling, pretty muchstraight line up to this point."

Then he went into how dynamite came along and how burning rates changed, and we went beyond just making fire; now we could make explosions – the "New Boom Fire." He worked his way to the chain reaction that was like the New Boom Fire, only cubed about five hundred times over and measured by how many New Boom Fires were in one reaction.Not only could this fire produce a mega explosion, but it could also produce a cloud that ate up everything under it – "The GigEnding Fire." Taking it to the point that if you want to talk about fire, you have to look at it and realize it comes in three different flavors: Original, New Boom, and Gig Ending.

The Pipe pointed out how these fires and Uncle Albert and Uncle John fit together. "See, Uncle Albert and Uncle John caught fire when it went from a straight line to a curve. Not many cats catch bottom to top, a line like this. They saw the burning rates change. Naz already done water, based on what we've done to the burning rates not hard to figure what's coming next." It was a theology speculating the end would come this way and by our hand, not God's. God's hand is in His pocket. He already knows the end.

Seemed everything came in sets of three with the Pipe. It was like he personally knew every cat that he had ever read. There was something biblical about him, but he didn't hold toone trinity but had several. And looking back, you had to deal with him on three different levels. He had a level where the dark side was greater than the light, a level where they were even, and a level where the light was greater than the dark side.I probably caught him when he was even, but I've talked to other cats that have caught the other sides, and they've got theirraps.

But Stovepipe's ability to just put thoughts in your head and not take one side or the other was his greatest gift of all the gifts he had. He could blend *Genesis* with the "Big Bang," taking what he liked from both and filling the rest in with cats that did and didn't exist. Taking the position that if they didn'texist, they should have. Anytime you caught a full-blown rap from the Pipe, you felt you picked up more than any other cat.He could pack your head and let you draw your own conclusions, right or wrong. He made everything fit no matter how far out in left field. That was the problem.

That day, by the time we made the parking lot, Vern and Ida, Boxcar Willie, Lord Buckley, Stonewall Jackson, and William Tecumseh Sherman, along with Albert Woolson and John Salling and anyone else mentioned, were all packed in theback seat of that '63 Comet. Thought about it over the years, but never really talked about it again, except when telling someother cat about the Pipe and all the conclusions I've drawn. After lunch that day, seems there wasn't anything I didn't know about the Stovepipe. And in passing, it wasn't until several years later I learned Stonewall's own boys took him outat Chancellorsville, at night while he was riding the line,checking up on them. If he was an Ohio boy, he was on the wrong side, pretty much how lunch went that day.

******

Had a lot blowing through my wig as the sun began to set that day. We walked through the parking lot, and Pipe fired up the Comet. My thoughts left me as soon as I noticed thedashboard lit up like a Christmas tree, something that went unnoticed in the light of day. There wasn't a warning light that wasn't on, and it concerned me, but not Pipe.

He put the Comet in gear and then asked me a favor. Wanted me to catch a tape he made with a group of guys known as the *Big Notes* once we made Akron. Backed her up, put her in gear, and we headed up the road, Pipe filling me in on an album he had finished, while I kept my eyes on the dashboard lights, amazed we were moving. After a while, I got to whereI liked the colors. With every mile we made, my concern beganto fade.

It was original work. At the time, I knew this was big, and not until recently how big. Up until that point, anything you heard from the Stovepipe was live, and that was just him sittingin with any band in town. Up to that point, the Pipe never had a band. There wasn't an instrument he feared; he could play them all. Wasn't a song he couldn't sing. There wasn't a college bar in a five-state area that wouldn't be pleased as hellto put out that the Stovepipe was sitting in at their place tonight.

The hour, hour and a half, it took to make Akron was filledwith a cast of new characters as Stovepipe broke down each one of the *Big Notes*. Characters in a band that I eventually heard but never saw, again a conclusion drawn several years after the fact, and at the time, before we reached Akron, I couldrattle their names off like John, George, Paul, and Ringo. Now, I'm hard-pressed to come up with even one name.

Pipe rapped on as we drove. Told me the first time he ever played in public was while sitting in with a band called The *Scouts* when he was about ten years old. "Yeah, I was in The Scouts for a little while," Pipe chuckled. "Played strings for a couple of sets, then keyboards, then drums, horns, played every instrument they had in the house one night, and a few pulled from the trunks of the cars parked outside. Ten years old, and no one seemed to care; they only cared about the tunes. It all started on the Ohio River, Marietta. Can't remember the name of the bar, but I remember playing in front of maybe ten or more cats, but not much more than that." He then noted since then he'd played bigger crowds and better instruments, but he always loved that size crowd. He lit a smoke and then mumbled, "From that night on, it all changed."

He then went on to tell me about the music, women, and beer that he got an eight-year jump on back in what he called his "3.2 Era" - back when 3.2 beers covered the interval of time between eighteen and twenty-one, along with the chicks that fill the era. "Three two beer, three two bars, and three two chicks, yeah, I liked that junior varsity juice back then, opened a lot of doors for me, kind of put me on the map. When I played, they'd pop them open; I certainly got my cut." He had such a provocative way of putting it you almost found yourself subconsciously dropping an 'n' in the last word.

He footnoted the times and his youth. "Yeah, the tunes took my age, along with some other stuff. I'd put them out there, and no one cared how old I was. Hell, when I was ten, I was really twenty." Went on about his miss-spent youth for another twenty minutes, right down to the old candle lit at both ends and how he burned up the things he would be needing down the road. And if that era taught him anything, it was that he had better slow down and save his strength.

But that was back when Stovepipe played other cat's music, working the instruments developing his voice. I thought about this, and I became aware of how important this ride was as I tuned Pipe out for a few moments. This ride was going to dropme off in a part of town no other cat had ever been. The Pipe was going to take me to a whole new intersection with his name and music on all the street signs. And one thing was for sure, Pipe wasn't sitting in anymore. No, Pipe was now producing and recording his own tunes, and I was going to be the one tocatch it, ground floor.

It was huge, and a lot of cats can rap on without end about Stovepipe's *Save Your Strength* album. Some say they've got the album, I've never seen the album, and it's not like I haven'tspent a lot of time trying to track it down. No, that night, I hearda tape from a big old reel-to-reel Wollensak tape recorder. I never heard the vinyl album. But they say they're out there.

I came close a few years back. Thought I found it at a yardsale in Paint, Ohio. The guy had a basket of albums, and there it was, Popeye lying back in a hammock, pipe in hand, squeezing down a can of beer like a can of spinach, the tattoo font spelling it all out—*Save Your Strength*— with a white background, black letters, gray lines silhouetting the Popeye backdrop. All the songs were on the back; all of them started coming back. Heart pounding, I picked it up, paid the man, andwas out of there in a flash. I just grabbed it and booked. I didn'tcheck a thing there. Got home, took the album out of the jacket,turns out to be Lawrence Welk. All I have as proof is the jacket. All I can tell you is what it held.

******

I can pinpoint *Save Your Strength* to the home of Starlite Smoot in the harsh part of south Akron, down by the rubber shops, right by the tracks, off South Main. The outside of her house wasn't anything like the inside. The house was worn and beat up on the outside, but inside, there was soft light where it felt warm and smelled clean.

Our entrance into her home was effortless. The place was covered with books, most of them on music, the rest political, some history, no magazines or newspapers, one TV and one radio. The furniture was eclectic, to say the least, silhouetted against different colored walls of purple, pink, yellow, and orange. None of the furniture was bought but made for her by friends. It all fit together to provide the perfect atmosphere forwhat was to happen.

For a first-time meeting, the atmosphere was relaxed, and the conversation on how we'd just missed the *Big Notes*, who were all just there maybe fifteen minutes before we made her door. Physically, she wasn't a particularly beautiful woman, but she was far from plain. Her attraction came from a gentle magnetism that few people possess, and in short, we were introduced, talked for a while, and then she disappeared. Haven't seen her since, haven't forgotten her either. If I ever do see her again I feel I could go up to her and start talking to her right where we left off without skipping a beat; she wasthat easy to talk to.

There wasn't a bad seat in the house, as Stovepipe began towork the reel-to-reel and the kitchen at the same time. His rhythm showing up before the sound as Pipe moved around theroom and into the kitchen, grabbing an ashtray here and there, placing them strategically for max convenience. A large bag of chips hit the coffee table, with a backup bag of pretzels and then two large quarts of bottled beer right behind the bags. Notone, but four packs of smokes hit the coffee table, regular and menthol, filtered and unfiltered, along with a fat jay; everything that night was on the

Pipe. The lights were broughtdown, the switch flipped on the reel-to-reel, and the rest of thenight set aside to catch what the Pipe had put down for the firsttime ever in max comfort.

First five to ten seconds, nothing but dead tape, and then I caught the first cut, and afterwards, you could've knocked meover with a feather. But that first cut wasn't anything like the next cut, and the cut that followed, and the cut that followed that cut, or the next. I heard: *"The Big Gig,' "Gravy and Grease," "Cat In The Box," "War Midgets," "Won A Lotta Battles – Lost A Lotta Wars," "Take and Hold," and "Move Less And Think More."*

What is the effect? To this day can't listen to an instrumental beginning like *Give Me Shelter,* for example, without going back to that night, and as great as that beginningis, it pales in comparison to what I heard on *Save Your Strength.* It's like that with a lot of other tunes, too. In fact, every great tune I've heard since that night is like something I've heard before, only not as strong, not as clean, and not as good. And in a way, I'm not really sure if the Pipe did me a favor or not since that night. Tunes have been hard on me, never quite getting me to where I once was.

Been times in the past where I've wondered if it really wasn't some sort of a set up—Stovepipe putting on me the *BigNotes,* then Starlite Smoot putting on me how the *Big Notes* just left before we made the door.

I remember that night and what I heard, I'm now one of those cats putting out the Pipe played every instrument on *Save Your Strength;* there are no Big Notes.

I don't care what I've said in the past because the Pipe wasgood enough to play with tape. It was one thing to catch the Stovepipe's presence, but it was completely something else to catch his timing. He didn't leave to other cats where to jump in and where to jump out; he stitched that tape together himself.

I'm thinking there's just Pipe on that album.

Over the years, I've had to come to some hard conclusions. No doubt Stovepipe was the son of Vern and Ida, and we know where Vern and Ida come from. And if déjà vu is something happening before, happening again, then Pipe ran it in reverse where something happened again having happened before.

It was little more than coincidence that the first cut that night, "Gravy and Grease," was about lunch at a truck stop. In fact, the whole *Save Your Strength* album is about the afternoon I spent with him right up to getting in his sixty-three Comet with all our buddies and blowing up the road to Akron.

To this day, how he pulled this off gasses me even more than the tunes.

And the cold hard fact is that I never caught the Pipe live anywhere; the stuff I've put out in the past about hearing him live comes from the cats to the base of ten who have caught Pipe live and told me about it. I never caught a live note from the cat, only a recording that, to this day, I still believe was all Stovepipe, but who knows? Another cold hard fact is I only caught Stovepipe for one day, and never again, the day I left Athens heading for Columbus, but winding up in Akron. And the last cold hard fact is that if you measured the distance from what is and isn't, you'd find Stovepipe right in the middle.

No two ways about it; the Pipe was gifted and knew how to play the real and the unreal. Heard a while back he blew out a few years ago. Heard also that after a while he only played one note, an "E," that everybody waited for on the stuff he put out later. Blew it from some organ pipe he ripped out of some church and then had some cats bend his tune around the note. Eventually, Pipe wanted to save his notes just like he wanted to save his strength. Some say he went from 180 to 400 pounds; he liked those truck stops. Died on a bus one night after realizing he'd spent what he wanted to save.

Album 2: Bagpipes and Bongos (According to Noose)

I've heard everything out there about Stovepipe. I caught "Move Less and Think More," first album, last cut. Only I didn't get the concentrated dose, like some, probably caught Stovepipe ninety-six times, that when added up, comes to about twenty-four hours spread over about three months and sixteen days, not counting weekends.

For five days a week, the Pipe was my clock. And the Pipe wasn't anything about saving his strength. When I caught him, he was all light and dark, weight and vibration, fission and fusion, bagpipes and bongos, like he had something to prove.

I was a twilight student at the university located in the center of Ohio, the big one. Took my classes late, worked for meals at a sorority house, and worked for money punching computer cards at the institute south of campus. That was my productive side; unfortunately, my unproductive side far outweighed it. I had some issues on the edge: bad grades, a determined draft board, a warrant for my arrest, and a love affair. This is what was in my suitcase when we banged into each other in 1969.

And when that happened, and the Pipe caught these four edges, he picked the last one to smooth. He liked love affairs. Pointed out, you get your choice with love affairs – some people love people, some people love places, some people love things. And whatever you choose to love, it's usually at the expense of the other two. That's why love affairs are usually doomed from the start. No matter what you choose or how hard you try, one of the three is always out of balance. "What kind you got?" So I started to unload all I had going on with this chick, and that's when Pipe started calling me "Noose," and itstuck.

Actually, the first five times we crossed paths really don't count. Never said anything at the bus stop we shared one winter, five days a week, after dark. Looking back, the Pipe gotabout five free days of advertising, me telling other cats about this Amish Beatnik at the bus stop, top to bottom. About the sixth night, I broke the ice, not so much by asking him about the patch that covered his one eye, but more by asking him what was up with the musical note that was on the patch.

The open eye he had had the power of two, and I was being stared down by a one-eyed jack. He came back with, "This is where I keep my notes; I catch a lot with one headlight." He then went on about his eye, and by the time he was through, he had successfully explained how a limit could be expanded, where having one eye can actually be better than having two.

A lot of cats out there will tell you Stovepipe just goofed on people with the patch, but I'm one putting down Pipe needed the patch to see the notes. Like one eye was method, and the other application, like one eye was for writing and theother for playing. He was way beyond the curve covering left brain/right brain thinking. In short, his eyes were like the knobs on the radio; you don't use both of them at the same time; youuse one to turn on and the other to tune in.

See, when Stovepipe wasn't carrying an instrument when he was putting down music, written music, the note was over his left eye. When Pipe played and carried, the note was over the right eye. I picked this up about mid-winter of that year. That's how long it took me to get, "What's up with the note?"This, and the fact that

Stovepipe never liked looking at the world with both eyes. "With all that goes down on this crazy swinging sphere," as he liked to put it, one eye was enough. "Dig! We see more than we need to with one head light." He called his condition "Motorcycle Eye."

At the time, the engine in my head was right for the octane the Pipe put out. I filled up every night at the bus stop. He'd check out what I had going on under my hood, mess with the wires, and send me on my way. Stovepipe and the bus stop became so magnetic that as soon as it started getting dark, I was always there with a little light to spare.

******

Pipe never made the stop before me. I was always early. Liked to watch him turn the corner and glide the half block to the stop. Had a cool nod for every cat he passed. Had a straight gait, but he could spin and weave. Never tripped or stumbled once. I caught him ninety-six times in all kinds of weather. He had a physical presence and could handle a smoke; he could hit the storm sewer every time with every butt he ever flicked, always from about ten feet out, no matter what, never missed.

Had that prophet look and wore a long coat that covered a dress shirt with a thin tie, his dress pants tucked into his rubber boots, capped it off with a nice thin-brimmed fedora. At the time, the hat was gray, the coat was black, the shirt was white, the tie was gray, pants and boots were black. The only three colors he knew. After a while, you put together he had three coats, three pairs of pants, three shirts, three ties, three pairs of boots, and three hats. He even had white rubber boots. Factor the number of colors along with the types of attire, and you can come up with over a hundred different combinations.

He had a different look for the time. The time when Navy peacoats, and Army field jackets, plaid flannel shirts, worn jeans, sandals, beads, long hair, and beards filled the landscape. Pipe's look for the time was more uniform. A look that conveyed whatever he was doing, he was serious about it. I guess the best description of the look – a white Malcolm X.

Pipe played a lot of color combinations with these three colors that winter, and that's kind of how our time would pass, in combination: three minutes of me telling him where I was at and twelve minutes of him bending something around it. And where I was always the first to arrive, the Pipe was always the first to speak. "We tight or loose tonight, Noose?" He could say those six words at just the right tempo and with just the right inflection to make them sound like a foreign language, a language only you and he could pick up.

******

Remember we talked sports once, as an icebreaker in the beginning. Pipe dug the Bucks, knew their stats, and went on, "It's all about getting down field. Cool, you're at a place that understands this. Gotta move past whatever's in front of you. Easy to figure out, hard to do, do it right, it's a ball, it's the big gig." Went on like this for some time, and by the time he finished, I felt like I'd caught the best half time speech ever given and from appearance by the last cat that would give it.

By the time Pipe rolled it up, you got the feeling; hell, Woody probably knew the Pipe, along with the Bear; who knows? I've caught the rap out there about how they both recruited him, but that's a whole different story. Point being he was as tight with athletics as he was with tunes.

In fact, it was right after the Pipe's half time speech that I set up in my mind that I'd be making that bus stop every night but two, no matter what. So it isn't like the Stovepipe didn't make a contribution to what I had going on. Every day seemed to start an album side earlier. Found myself showing up ahead instead of behind to class and work. Found early worked better than late, and to get my fix, certain hoops had to be jumped through. The rhythm of the day hinged on what was said right after dark by the Pipe. I started owning the day because he owned the night.

I was getting it down, and early on, I picked up that talking about school right at the end of my three minutes always left me with something that could be either written or calculated that fit right in with some class the following day. It was spooky. So as the winter drifted away that year in white, gray, and black, my grades improved, the draft board seemed to back off, and the ticket seemed to go away, leaving the third edge, love.

******

Love, the three-way split between people, places, and things, is all about balance. Each has its own specific gravity and orbit. Put a little bit more into one, and it throws the other two out of orbit. Pipe broke it down to me pretty much that way the first time the topic ever came up.

This was right after I told him about a recent weekend event I had, covering where she and I were on the map. Told him about driving over two hundred miles to see her, getting to the place, only to get dumped on some more, thinking the thing to do is drink my tits off and leave a wake of destruction in two or three towns on my way back. I told him about people, places and things, her, the towns, the beer. "She turned my ride into an alcohol-fueled rocket. They made my plates in each town, and everyone wants me back; they're dead serious about this. In fact, if it wasn't for her, we wouldn't be having this conversation."

Winter was just settling in when this took place. The temperatures were starting to sting, and the white was giving way to a hard, gray slush brought on by constant thawing and freezing, where it was either too warm or too cold to snow. Looking back at early winter that year, Pipe was in contrast with the new snow, going about two-thirds black in his attire. Mid-winter was two-thirds gray, and late winter two-thirds white. Pipe was an environmentalist, only to the point that he could cruise through any environment. Part of that inside blessing other cats talk about. And these changes in attire didn't happen at once; they were gradual and only came to your attention most of the time as an afterthought.

The night I brought the Pipe in on this chick that was tearing my wig apart, the gradual could no longer go unnoticed. In earlier bus stop encounters, I had touched on her, but Pipe wasn't ready to hear about it or give it any attention until the right color transition had been made to gray. After the transition, the Pipe filled me in.

And where a lot of cats know the patch game, not a whole lot know about how Stovepipe played the wedding band.

Seems the first part of winter, Pipe worked his smoke with fine leather gloves, he called them his "safe crackers." The night I brought up the rampage this woman was putting on me, during my three minutes, was the night the safe crackers came off, and I caught the wedding band.

That was the first and last time. From that point on, I consciously never looked at either hand again, except for really, really short glimpses. Over time, it seemed I couldn't catch the band like the first time.

Was he married? Two-thirds of my head is nodding up and down. Know her name and seen her picture. And I know she was definitely in the three-way split for the Pipe's love. I also know there are some cats out there with their head moving side-to-side; guess it depends on who you talk to. I've caught their rap, married or not, every cat agrees he had a woman, or better yet, she had him.

He called her "The Rib," dark hair, dark eyes, and not hard to look at. The picture he showed me, she was completely clothed, but I saw her naked. Compared to the lineage Spoon puts out about the Pipe, she was a real thoroughbred; the word "illegitimate" is not in her resume.

Her people came from the Wyoming territory, where women's suffrage was first granted in 1869. She had a direct line to Victoria Claflin Woodhull, who in 1872 was the first woman candidate for president, nominated by the National

Women's Suffrage Association, National Radical Reformers Ticket. But all that didn't matter; she could've come from some whore house outside some military base, and it wouldn't have changed how Pipe felt about her.

After a while, I found the orbits of the three-way split for Pipe weren't any different from the orbits and splits I had going on. This was the beginning of *Bagpipes and Bongos.* The cats that tell you it's his weakest album don't get the Pipe.

******

The Rib could take you right through the Women's Movement, and from what the Pipe put down, you got the feeling she was the female equivalent of the Pipe. She had the same type of power Eve had when she got Adam to bite the apple. After *Save Your Strength,* there wouldn't be six following platters without her.

The Rib understood the wind, the weight, and the vibration behind it. She knew where it came from, and she could hear where it was going. She did research on the Beaufort Wind Scales.

What she wanted to do was to take the two most distant sounds from each other and blend them together to come up with a new element in sound based on the Beaufort Wind Scale. And she didn't want Stovepipe to play; she wanted Pipe to write.

One early midwinter, right after a dark encounter, Pipe put the domestic scene of both of them cleaning their place. Put it down to the point, I felt I was right there with them, picking up a few newspapers. The Rib made percolated coffee while the Pipe vacuumed.

Gradually, Pipe was able to blend the terse sound of the vacuum cleaner with the rhythmic popping of the coffee maker to come up with the new element of sound The Rib was looking for. You couldn't find two more distant sounds, and Pipe blended them. A big requirement had been filled at that point in her life when Pipe did this subconscious requiem, and she was overcome with passion.

The carpets got clean that night, and Pipe went on about the discussion the two had about what two instruments could produce the sound of a vacuum cleaner and a coffee maker. By breakfast, after an extremely really friendly night of connecting in more ways than one, they came up with bagpipes and bongos. That's when the big experiment began.

Pipe thought it was a cool idea for down the road, but The Rib wanted it now. He tried to play it off by telling her, "Together, we're the best sound two instruments can make - You and me."

Pipe was comfortable with what he was putting out, but she got him to move in her direction when she told him it was just a matter of time before what he was putting out would be old, fat, and bald. Got Pipe to buy into the fact that if he was for real, he could pull it off. There is a lot of Adam and Eve in *Bagpipes and Bongos.* Had a place, two people, and an apple Stovepipe really didn't want to bite.

From the beginning, the ground rules were set: just two instruments and the best sound one could get from them through written Beaufort. Every night that midwinter, he had a new episode of what was becoming a struggle. Caught up in trying to reproduce the sound he put down one night while goofing around with a vacuum cleaner and a coffee maker. The Rib set up the conflict within him. Had him thinking - he had it once, could he get it again? Secondly, once he got it, could he expand it? No two ways The Rib got him to bite.

The dialog Pipe put down about the two was right from the "Garden." The Rib beguiled with the idea of creating something new, just like Eve buying into becoming like God if she ate the apple. And The Rib was all about what if the woman would have pulled it off and became God. She operated from that square.

Mid-winter was deep cold that year but not cold enough to hold my attention; the Pipe owned that. Never noticed the cold that much going to or coming from the bus stop. I do remember everyone bitching about it, but it was something I was beyond.

All that held my interest was what Stovepipe was going to lay on me next. And where other cats that I know well, who've crossed paths with the Pipe, put on me about how the South won the Civil War, I have how the Pipe broke it down to me one night that God is a woman.

"Dig!" Pipe began. "There were people, places, and things in the Garden of Eden, and that was the last time the three were in perfect orbit. After the incident with the apple, *bang*! Everything went out of orbit. The apple was the 'Big Bang' everyone was rapping about. Free will stuck right in the middle of the knowledge of good and evil. After the Lord saw two bites out of His apple, he put it on them. Told the Dust and the Bone – 'you want to mess with the orbits? I'm going to show you how hard perfect is'. From that day on, he left the two and the rest of us poor cats with a lot of broken and smashed hearts because we can't make the orbits right, no matter how hard we try."

Looking back, the twist Pipe had on the Garden was like the music he was trying to write in Beaufort. He was trying to blend the Garden with outer space, or something like it, I don't know. But he went on that what the Lord put on us after the two bites from His apple was physics. He then lit a smoke and exhaled. "We can figure motion out, we can calculate it, but we sure as hell can't control it. Like you can see the train wreck coming, know it's going to be rough, double rough, but you can't stop it once it goes into motion, there's your big bang."

Within fifteen minutes of that night in the winter of that year, the Pipe got me to thinking of God and the possibilities, not to where if He did or didn't exist, but to whether He might be a female. To this day, when I don't have anything in particular blowing through my mind, I grapple with the concept and still haven't put it to bed. And this should give youcats some weight to size up about fifteen minutes after dark encounters with Stovepipe, and also let you know why the coldnever got to me that winter.

And as time evolved that night, Pipe broke sex down to me."You got the male sex, the female sex, and connected sex; connected sex is the best. God, the great plumber, knows thereain't any plumbing without the male and female connection. Got to ask yourself, when we're connected what are we? Male or female? That's why connected sex is the best because we're neither. See, man came from dust, woman came from man's rib, and when men and women connect, it comes from two desires - the desire to put the bone in touch with its original owner or the original owner's desire to be in touch with the bone. The attraction is all about the bone, who has it, and whowants it."

******

The next night, Pipe rapped about how his work was goingand touched upon The Rib. I can't recall any of what he said, only the realization he loved her mentally and physically. And the conclusion was drawn that where the Pipe's influence is legendary, if not mythical, it wasn't like there wasn't someoneout there that couldn't influence the Stovepipe.

In fact, it got to the point I began to figure out that the rap I was getting was a second hand rap played by the Pipe but produced by The Rib. To take it a step further, Pipe was starting to transfigure into being The Rib. It was so close to having happened that to this day, two-thirds of me saw it that night, while one-third tells me it never happened.

Seems God had no sexual orientation until the apple was bitten. Fact is, the sex of God was actually determined by the first bite and the person who made it. And it wasn't so much that the woman got the man to take a bite, but it was more in the light that with a second bite, she was willing to share.

Pipe pointed out that Eve didn't do anything different from what a man would have done had he had the first conversation with the snake. Boiling and steaming it to where a lot of cats put the whole thing on the women, when in reality it came down to the fact that there was one apple and two bites, and there was one punishment and two people, the punishment like the apple had to be shared.

To take it a step further, since the woman came from the man's rib, it was actually the male part of the female that gave into the temptation. It was when we reached this point that I started to pick up on the visual transfiguration. It wasn't Pipe in drag; it was her.

She lit a smoke and exhaled. "Dig! Man provided the main ingredient. A lot of cats hold that because this woman is basically man-made. Boom! Take a little snooze; next thing you know, you're short a rib, and we got somebody new hanging in the garden. Hell, Adam wasn't anything more than a supply depot." She or he went on and on about the creation of women, winding and tumbling to some foregone conclusion that would usually set your wig on fire.

That conclusion being, one way or the other, if God is either man or woman, it means one sex or the other is out numbered, it means one sex is more like God than the other, it means one sex is better than the other, and getting a handle on the concept becomes important, no matter what sex you are.

The following night, the artificial light coming from the headlights and streetlights provided a nice contrast against the gray buildings and clear dark sky. The piercing cold put form to every breath taken, and when you spat, what came out of your mouth bounced off the sidewalk like a dropped marble. It was cold enough to make what is often unbreakable, brittle, and very breakable, and because of this, our wait for the bus was a little longer than usual.

It was also the night Pipe showed up with a nice slender long box with a fine, dyed leather strap attached to it, slung over his shoulder like a rifle. He had a different look that was subtle, and I eyeballed him for a while until it hit me that I was catching the Stovepipe's left eye for the first time ever, and the winter solstice of *Bagpipes and Bongos* was upon us.

From that point on, the Pipe was going to be playing what he'd put down in written Beaufort. The note had relocated, and he'd catch the rest of winter with the left eye, his "playing eye."

Wanted to ask him about the box, didn't get to any of it that night because Pipe had me wrapped up from the night before with God, and which sex was out numbered. The cold made it so that every word that came from his mouth came in bursts of white, giving them some sort of visual authority. And it wasn't a problem to return to yesterday's topic and continue where he left off as he put down how it might be.

Stovepipe began by pointing out that God created just two populations that can only reproduce one or the other andnothing in between. Populations of races, age, religion, geographic location, and so on, are totally secondary measurements of the two 'true' populations. Only the male and female populations are the populations that count. He then let the smoke held in his left-hand drop to the ground and steppedon it, and without missing a beat, continued, "About the only thing you have on God is the burning bush that told Moses, 'Iam.' It's hard to tell the sex of fire."

Without hesitation, he lit another smoke that accented the weight of what he was about to put down. "The big assumptionis that women are outnumbered; God is on man's side, but I don't know. See, to our way of thinking, God has to be one orthe other because our wigs can't hold anything in between." Hethen ran his right thumb up and down the strap holding the boxon his shoulder and, for a brief moment, appeared very apprehensive. Turned his head in a way where you could catchhis whole face and shot out, "If God has to be one or the other,he's probably a woman - it just might be it came down to the first bite."

Now, Pipe might have bought into this, but it ran contrary to my thinking at the time. Initially, it wasn't enough, but as Pipe rolled on, he got me off that square and onto the square where, to this day, it's still a mystery to me. He said a lot aboutthe concept, but what stuck in my mind was how he pointed out that more women than men are born, that they live longer,and have a far better record than men when it comes tocompassion, ending with, "The 'angel of the battlefield.' During our main stay, civil drag. Sure as hell wasn't any man.The Red Cross is female."

Pipe didn't stop there. "That part about 'He sent His only begotten Son' was written by a man with only one frame of reference: his sex. It could have come down just as easily, 'She sent Her only begotten Son,' had a woman first put that stroke to paper. End of subject, subject closed." Pipe was convinced, but he could never get me off the middle square.

Taking a step back, what I got that night was the theology behind *Bagpipes and Bongos*. That the two distant sounds, the two different instruments, represented the two true populations, and the trick was to get the best sound that could possibly be produced by each of them together. And that was the key word - "together." Just these two instruments, with nothing in between, written in Beaufort to get this sound.

Back then, everything he was doing was so new and different. There weren't any other cats out there attempting a new scale on a diametric population to create not a new sound but the best sound. It was the marriage of two instruments; one pounding, the other squeezing, trying to find this sound.

******

The following night, I finally got to the box Stovepipe had hanging over his right shoulder. Told me Mooney Warther, out of New Philly, made it for him like that was some type of a big deal. And it was in a way, because that box, after looking at it closely, was damn near perfect - had that breakdown pool cue look, gray strap, lot of coats of black lacquer, lot of white ivory inlay. It became an even bigger deal later on when I found out who Mooney Warther was (He's another story).

Pipe laid on me that there was no point in guessing what

instrument the box held, but that didn't stop me as I eyeballed it for a while. The only thing that came to me was the box had the same dimensions and volume of two, two-by-fours, about four feet long, nailed together. And the Pipe was right; I didn't have a clue as to what instrument was in the box.

Turns out it really wasn't an instrument, but part of an instrument, a section of organ pipe in 'E.' Turns out the Beaufort scale originated from the amount of wind-blown air put through a two-and-one-half-inch diameter, four- and- half foot tube ripped out of some pipe organ. These amounts are measured and marked in new notation. The notation being universal to any instrument, which, when read and played or sung correctly, would produce the best sound of instrument and voice.

Pipe rolled on, "See, once you blow an 'E' from the tube, you have bedrock. The 'E' is the key. You, Beaufort, as you come up from the rock and build on the 'tube note' based on the steam put behind it. Once you get the Beaufortization down, you decide what instruments you want to wrap around the tune."

There was plenty more of what he was putting down, and he took it to the point that, for sure, he was the only cat on the planet that understood what he was doing because shortly after the part about instrument selection, he totally lost me, but it didn't seem to matter. And it wasn't a case where he had a disinterested audience; it was more a case where he was way beyond his audience.

The following nights of that winter were bound tightly around what was before him, the two distant sounds and the woman behind them. Nothing Pipe did before or after had the effort he put behind *Bagpipes and Bongos*. He came to the conclusion the album would have just two cuts, one featuring one instrument, or sex, over the other. Side A would be all bagpipes with the bongos in the background; Side B would beall bongos with the bagpipes in the background. Each cut abouta half hour long.

During our rap on this approach, I broke it down to Pipe that each cut would probably be a lifetime supply of those two instruments for most people. Pipe didn't take the comment well. The thought of him putting something out there that every cat in tunes didn't want some part of was foreign to the wavesrunning through his wig.

But in the end, that's pretty much how it turned out. And for the tune makers that caught it, after it arrived, it kind of became the 'Niagara Falls tight rope of albums.' Where the guy walking the rope over the falls gasses everyone, but it's not something every cat is going to run out and try to do. And thisbugged Pipe.

The fact there are maybe one in a million cats that can do the rope over the falls was secondary to Pipe. The whole effortdidn't mean a thing if the tune makers didn't pick it up. One ofthe reasons he always backed away from *Bagpipe and Bongos* whenever it came up. Once it was finished, he didn't like talking about it.

******

Then, one night, the snow returned - came in at an angle, sticking to everything. The traffic slowed to where one could walk faster than the traffic could move. From the stop, Pipe andI watched the traffic, both commenting how the cars were like some hurt animal struggling to keep moving, to keep up with the herd, refusing to die.

With each flake that fell, the struggle became more and more difficult, but to me, it wasn't without some merit as the idea of blowing off work started swirling like the snow throughmy head. At about the same time this thought came to me, Pipe offered an invitation to travel with him that night. It was like he read my mind, and without hesitation, I lit a smoke and nodded okay.

I went to the pay phone across the street and called off.

In the distance, the bus fought its way to us like some large insect surrounded by an army of hungry ants, finally sliding to a stop in front of us. It was the bus Pipe took that headed north. The door opened, and I got on with him. I don't remember seeing the driver, but I am sure he was there. What I rememberis we were the only two on the northbound; we had it all to ourselves.

With the exception of the first light, the trip seemed more like we were flying instead of riding - flying not so much like in a plane, but more like a blimp, in fair weather, slow and smooth. The ride wasn't anything like the weather outside. Outside, everything was starting to lose control; there was a fender bender every block, but inside, we felt safe and warm. In fact, it was the most surrealistic ride I've ever taken.

But at the first light, the bus had to maneuver to miss a herd of stuck cars, and the briefcase Pipe was carrying, which I never noticed before, that just seemed to appear out of nowhere, flew from his lap, and his papers poured onto the floor. Calmly, Pipe muttered, "Thought I latched it."

Actually, they weren't papers, but "a" paper on two sticks—a scroll. One end managed to roll clear to the end of the bus. Pipe took the end closest to where we were sitting; I traveled the length of the bus to get to the other end.

As I moved down the aisle, I gazed at what was on the floor, and it came to me that what I was looking at was the written Beaufort. Outside of The Rib, I was probably the first person to ever see it. I don't know how to read music, but I know written music when I see it, and this wasn't anything like the written music we are all used to seeing, not even close. The Beaufort, if anything, was far more visually pleasing, its symbols more like the runes from some ancient manuscript found in some long-forgotten Celtic tomb or tomb of that nature. It was writing that had some order and purpose to it, butat the same time unknown.

The placement of symbols left one not knowing if it was read left to right or right to left, bottom to top or top to bottom,only that it was written with an incredibly steady hand and influenced by an equally incredible mind.

At the time, I didn't see myself on a bus but in a tunnel leading to some unknown chamber that was at the one end of this long scroll, a wizard at the other end, paying little or no attention to my presence. As I concentrated on what was on the ground I became overwhelmed by the irony of seeing what feltlike it was part of the past when actually it is part of the future. Through it all, Pipe and the driver said nothing.

Next thing I can remember is coming to our stop andwaiting for people to get off the bus, where they came from, and when they got on a mystery, like the briefcase. The location we were at wasn't unknown to me; we were some place between the Venetian and the Blue Danube off High Street, where old houses and neighborhoods evolved into apartments occupied mostly by students. But we didn't wind up at a house or an apartment, but what was once an old neighborhood grocery store on a corner.

A musical grocery inside it was all acoustical. Had a centeraisle that displayed six rooms, three on each side. There were microphones and headsets in five of them. One had the reel toreels and control panels, all kinds of different color lighting, some stayed on, and others blinked. You felt like you were walking through a carnival.

What got recorded in this room would soon be pressed in vinyl. It was a place that was an old neighborhood on the outside but a new neighborhood on the inside.

It was a place where the ashtrays were heaped and the rest room small. It was a place I thought was unoccupied except for Pipe and myself until I saw a black woman come out of the restroom carrying a set of bongos. She entered the farthest room from us and began to play. She never said a word to either of us. Pipe and I entered another room; he opened the box, pulled out the "E Tube," turned on some equipment, had a smoke, rolled out the Beaufort, then blew the ceremonial note.

Next, he picked up a set of bagpipes and began to play. And after a harsh start, the distant bongos began to blend in with the pipes, like water running through some perfect plumbing. That night, I caught Side A: *Missing a Rib* and Side B: *I Got Your Rib,* and as far as I was concerned, the Pipe pulled it off together they both produced the best sound from each instrument to perfection.

Talking to Spoon about those days, the one thing we come up with that is real, is the black woman could only be South Akron Starlite Smoot, and that's about all.

Somewhere along the line, we've both caught raps from other cats, that when Stovepipe finally came to the conclusion God was a woman, The Rib came to the conclusion God was a man. And the way she put it on the Pipe was with the simple fact that every person walking the face of the earth was the direct result of a male orgasm. Telling Stovepipe, "Now you go ahead and tell me whose side God is on."

It caused quite a rub. For Pipe to put something in his wig for real and have The Rib tell him it's not real put a rift between them to the point they couldn't stay together. What was left was just blowing in and out each other's lives at different times and places, always trying to capture the best sound two instruments can make.

Didn't turn out any different for me; after some time, my wife left me, too. She took the album, last thing she got. I can see it under her arm. The album jacket with the diagonal line running from the bottom left corner to the top right corner, on the left, above the line, a picture of some bagpipes, on the right, below the line, a picture of some bongos. There's no writing; you have to figure it out. It appears like some fraction that has no common denominator. I haven't seen her or the album since she walked out the door; all she left me was the sales slip from C-Town Platters.

Its true Pipe blew out early and was overweight. It's also true he blew out on a bus, making his way back to The Rib, his female god. And that's pretty much *Bagpipes and Bongos.* Probably not his best work, but his strongest.

Album 3: Atomic Peanut (According to Motor)

I've pounded down a few drinks and smoked with those who knew Stovepipe. They'd bring Stovepipe up in just about every rap we've ever had on any topic. In fact, with these cats, the Pipe would always eventually bubble to the top. Figured I'd just hang around with them, and eventually, I'd bump into the Pipe. I would just 'Pipe On' with them until it happened.

None did the intro – I bumped into Stovepipe by chance. And when I did, it wasn't like I hadn't heard about the cat and what he was putting out. I heard enough about Stovepipe to know who he was when we first crossed paths, an advantage these cats never had, or so I thought.

Here's how it happened. A '63 Comet rolls into my station— well, it really wasn't my station, I was just working there—and rattles to a stop. Cat gets out wearing a gray ball cap, the black Beaver Cleaver jacket, Beach Boy cut white jeans, Chuck Taylor black low cuts trimmed out in white covering the feet, the shoes matching up perfectly with the patch covering his left eye.

I knew who he was from ten feet out, which was about the distance I first caught that white musical note on that black eye patch. I had him pegged from the start; I knew who he was. In the beginning, he didn't surprise me, but soon, that would change, and the day would become one surprise after another. I found out all the upfront knowledge I had on him really didn't matter. I wasn't going to be any different than any other cat that went one on one with him.

Looking back, I can tell you one thing: he was a whirlwind. First words out his mouth were, "You are a mechanic!" And it wasn't that he was asking you. It was more like he was *willing*you to be a mechanic.

Told him from square one not to let the surroundings fool him; all I did were gas tanks and windshields, and on rare occasions, a radiator cap and dipstick, and only if I was pushed. In short, my work was over the hood, not under it. Went on totell him he'd have to wait for Ernie, the real mechanic, and that could be anywhere from one to four hours since he'd just finished major surgery on the 66' Biscayne over by the bay. That, coupled with the fact it was a Friday afternoon, Pipe wasprobably looking more at four hours than one.

I was going to use the time to tell him everything I had on him from the other cats when Pipe barked, "Forget Ernie!" And then continued, "All we have to do is get this cat down that road. We don't need Ernie." He pulled a smoke and gazed at the road in front of the station the same way General Patton probably gazed at some German position, and you felt there was little difference between the two, the look letting you know what ever the obstacle, it was soon to be overrun.

From that point on, I've always felt as far as Pipe was concerned, he was okay with the four hours; it would be enough time to transform me into the mechanic he wanted. The timeframe didn't bother him at all.

Pipe then pulled down his gray ball cap to where you couldcatch the atomic symbol centered on the front of it. The radioactive symbol that I hadn't caught since the mid 50's it was quite the flashback, as my mind began to chant, "Run, Duck, and Cover" and I saw myself as an eight-year-old undersome wooden desk at school, safe and secure as long as I followed what I was being told. And that's how the Pipe was, "atomic," atomic at getting what he wanted.

The strange thing about the whole episode as it started to unwind was that he was demanding but not pushy. There's a difference. Pipe could throw the change up and get you to swing. Pipe played it that I was beyond gas tanks and windshields, that in a previous life, I invented the motor. "Let it all come back," Pipe urged.

And what was even stranger was from that point on it was like I'd never heard of Stovepipe, when in reality I had. I wanted to let him know that I had his number, knew who he was, knew about him from some other cats, but it all got lost in his rap about how I invented the motor in my other life.

Those other cats (who told me about him) became like Pipe; I couldn't pull any of them to mind to let him know I knew. In a way, it was like Pipe did some big rewind on a reel-to-reel and then hit erase. All my prior knowledge was gone, along with any advantage I thought I might have had over the other cats in dealing with him.

******

So, right from the start, I kind of entered this arena where I had all this buried knowledge of his work, his albums, *Save Your Strength*, and *Bag Pipes and Bongos,* and the cats that were around on the ground floor of each album dying to come out. But he had me subconsciously channel all of this energy right to the motor under the hood of that 63 red and white Comet. Anything I knew that day about anything was going right under the hood of that car.

At the time, late 60's early 70's, all I knew about rides was that they moved. What made them move, for all I knew, was magic. I was upfront with the Pipe from the beginning and told him, but he fired right back, "That's what we're tracking, baby! Magic! Make that ride roll!"

Next thing I know, a rap that started twenty feet from the red and white, by the time it ended ten minutes later, found me closing in on the hood. I began thinking maybe I did know more than I thought about motors. I began to feel a strange confidence.

If I was going to impress Stovepipe that day, it wasn't going to be with what I had on *Save Your Strength*, and *Bagpipes and Bongos,* or the story behind the patch, or the organ pipe in the box, and all the other stuff I had in the arsenal from the other cats.

No, if any impression was going to be made, it was going to come from my knowledge of the electrical, fuel, and hydraulics systems of the internal combustion engine that powered a '63 Comet. A knowledge that, in reality and in the kindest of terms, was very, very thin, almost nonexistent.

And looking back on all the cats that knew the Pipe, I'd have to say my claim to fame is that I was probably the first to make physical contact with Stovepipe. Right after I made the decision to play the situation through, I reached for the hood latch. Pipe brushed my right hand away with his left and held it, then grabbed my left shoulder with his right hand. At arm's length, he began, "Let me put some things down about this ride before you do your magic." And then began to squeeze. It was like being hooked up to battery cables, and I was being jumped.

I figured he was going to put down what the problems were, but instead, he put on me what a big slice of history I was dealing with.

He began, "This ride came together in 1963, a huge year." He then relaxed his grip. He went on to explain. The *Thresher* took the one-way dive in the North Atlantic that year, how it was the year of the artificial heart that got dropped in some cat somewhere and bought him an extra four days. He rolled into going from Pope John XXIII to Pope Paul VI, footnoting "The Pauls need seventeen more to tie." Nineteen sixty-three was also the year that school prayer ended.

At this point, Stovepipe went beyond the footnote, commenting, "Like prayer can be stopped. Prayer is one walkie-talkie you can turn on anytime, anywhere. It's a non- issue. Dig! What got stopped was the rote behavior that makes prayer meaningless. You've heard it said, and I believe it: *As long as there are tests, they'll be school prayer*. As long as there are tests, period, they'll be prayers. Doesn't have to be everywhere; it's already there. You can't stop prayer." And by the way he said it, you got the feeling he'd shot up a lot of them and knew what he was talking about.

After making his point, we both stood silent. We found ourselves lighting up to take the edge off, and with the first cloud of smoke that came from the Pipe, we returned to the year of manufacture as he exhaled. "Martin Luther King dropped 'I Have A Dream' on two hundred thousand cats in D.C. in '63. We hooked up the 'hot line' between Washington and Moscow, *The Feminine Mystique* came out in print and into our minds. By year's end, we had fifteen thousand military advisors in the rice paddies, and if that weren't enough, in the eleventh month of that year, they blew away JFK."

Pipe was notably out of smoke and out of breath when he ended, and I remember just looking at him and then at the Comet.

Not one word lost on me as he let go of my hand and shoulder, and I began to roll up my sleeves, and he let go of my left hand and took his hand from my right shoulder like you take a jumper cable from a battery. I'd been charged; it was mystical. I felt his voltage.

All that history behind it, plus the four to five years it had been on the road, left the 63 looking less than pristine. In fact, the Comet was some type of a metaphor of what happens as you get older and don't take care of yourself. It was a ride that looked and ran like it had been doing three packs of smokes and twelve packs of beer every day for a long time. Its body was getting heavy, and its motor was getting light. In fact, it looked like what the Pipe was starting to feel like, and that's why it was important to get it moving again. A lot of cats know me as "Motor," that handle came from the day I worked on Stovepipe's ride and has been with me ever since.

I don't even think my wife knows my real name. A lot of cats also put down that the Pipe never went to a doctor, which came from me. See, as that late afternoon moved on, the Pipe explained whenever he started feeling bad, the Comet would begin to run bad. Whenever he got the Comet fixed, he started to feel better. It was that simple: no need to see a doctor that somehow the car with all that history behind it and the Pipe shared some type of common karma. It was an unexpected blessing, Pipe explained, concluding that. "Although mechanics are expensive, they aren't anything like doctors," again footnoting, "Not only that, but mechanics probably know more work with more parts."

Pipe went on about this medical relationship: the head is the dash board, the heart is the carburetor, the stomach is the gas tank, the windshield eyes, and so on; the bones are the frame, the body the skin, to the point where after a while you naturally began to tune him out. You got the point.

I started to walk around the 63, inspecting it top to bottom. Taking in everything about it, I was like a fighter in the ring sizing up an opponent. What banged away at me the most was the junior varsity James Bond setup in the back seat to hold a reel-to-reel Wollensak like it was some type of permanent passenger. The topic of the similarities shared by people and cars changed when I asked, "What ya got here?" And he answered, "Maybe give you a taste later."

From that point on, a subconscious deal was struck between us. As soon as I started to move on the Comet, the tunes would start. That was the payoff. At that point, I figured it was time to get the motor running and get under the hood, if I was going to get into it. This time, when I went for the hood, the Pipe didn't stop me, and I went to work for him. I became his mechanic, or doctor, once I found out what I would get paid.

The big pull began in my mind to vacuum up everything I had on motors, and I began to trip out on automobiles. Seemed like every car I'd ever seen rolled through my wig, and that was about it. They just rolled by with little or no information.

And as hard as I focused, I was left with little or nothing, and then, in one strange and bizarre moment, the only question I could come up with about the 63 was… "What sex is it?"

For a moment, Pipe got that concerned look but then realized I didn't know where the question really came from or why I asked it. He then shook his head, laughed a little, and put on me, "No man, the Comet is like fire; it doesn't have a sex." Then, as an afterthought added, "If it has to have a sex – the way it's been acting – you know what sex."

After opening the hood, I got behind the wheel. The key was in the ignition. I turned it, and the 63 violently struggled to a start. Every warning light came; the dashboard showed a Whitman Sampler of problems. But despite the numerousstrange sounds that came from the motor, the Comet continuedto run. In fact, after a long time, the motor actually began to smooth out and sound semi-normal.

I got out of the car and stuck my head under the hood and watched the motor. There was grease and oil everywhere, but no fluids were shooting out, and the belts were moving. I cameto the conclusion the motor was a problem for down the road, another station, but wasn't the problem of the day.

I got back in the Comet to find the Pipe in the back seat, messing around with the reel-to-reel. Watched him from the rearview mirror, but he wasn't doing anything to hold my interest. What held my interest were the warning lights on the dashboard, there wasn't one that wasn't on. The whole situation, the smorgasbord of problems that came to light, brought on an ironic chuckle as I wryly smiled and shook my head.

Sat there for a while thinking, then put the Comet in gear and gave her the gas – nothing didn't move an inch. Gave her more gas right up to the point where the engine might blow, and then, out of nowhere, something caught and the Comet took off like a jet. It was all I could do to bring her under control as the Comet, Stovepipe, and I headed straight for the pumps.

It became one of those rare experiences where you see your

whole life flash in front of you and find yourself screaming. When we finally stopped, all that filled the windshield were the pumps, so close you could read the fine print on the inspection sticker. Another few inches and who knows how it might haveturned out, a few more inches and you'd be using his and my name in the past tense. It wigged me out, but the Pipe acted like it didn't happen, didn't say a word, and went back to messing with the Wollensak that came out of the whole incident like thePipe, unfazed.

It took more than one smoke for me to gather my composure, yet through it all, Stovepipe remained silent. Aftera while I put the Comet in reverse and backed up with no problem. Pipe broke the silence. "Hey, there ya go, pretty good. Now make reverse go forward." Like this shouldn't be hard. He made the comment as a confidence builder, like we were making progress, as I brought the car to a stop a little further than I'd planned, right at the entrance to the station.

Put the red and white in drive and stepped on the gas. Again nothing. It was stopped and completely blocking the entrance, which was just about maybe two hundred feet from a curve onthe road. Once you rounded that curve, you were practically ontop of the entrance.

The sweat was starting to come through my shirt, and my stomach was in knots as I began to realize the potential for disaster. Any cat coming around that curve and aiming for the station would be coming up on us before he and we knew it. Pipe and I would have to bank on the control of the situation coming from that cat's end because it sure wasn't going to be coming from our end.

And it wasn't like 33 out of Columbus didn't pick up some traffic. A ride probably blew by Ernie's once every two minutes. He knew what he was doing when he built the station. Ernie understood volume; probably one in every twenty pulled in.

It was just a question of time before one would want to pull in. But that was, on average, rides on that snake winding through Lancaster and Logan on into Athens traveled in packs. So, the scenario for an accident was skewed for more than two cars. If an accident were to occur, it more than likely wouldn't be just a two-car accident we would be creating; it would make the evening news a 'multi-car collision.' The scene kept blowing through my head, first the pumps, now the entrance. And I kept asking myself, "Why are you putting yourself through this for this cat?"

But then I began to think I'd been in similar situations, and my mind blew back into a five-paragraph field order, the mission being simple: Get the Comet out of the entrance and to a safe place, execute this with minimum movement and in a minimum amount of time.

Finally, some composure seemed to set in. So, without taking it any further, I put her in reverse and started to move.

Then it hit me: I was getting on 33 with only one gear, and I better stop and come up with a little more, like where to back up to, and what side of the road to be on. By backing up and then stopping, I managed to take a bad situation and make it worse.

Now half of the Comet was in the entrance and the other half on 33, a bigger and better target for the unsuspecting rounding the curve. You didn't have to be going to Ernie's to create a pile-up, that possibility was now open to the public.

What I failed to execute in the beginning was a survey of the terrain. Once I did, I found the option that had the least likely scenario for disaster turned out to be a figure eight. I'd back down two hundred feet to the used car lot, circle the lot, back down the same two hundred feet again, go around the pumps, and put the Comet right in front of Ernie's bay so he could get to it as soon as he got back. My work is finished.

As if missing the pumps earlier wasn't bad enough, right before I began 'operation figure eight,' Pipe and I got a real good preview of how things might turn out if lady luck decided against us. A big black New Yorker doing about sixty came barreling around the curve just moments before the operation got underway. Just as scripted, it seemed to come out of nowhere and was sure surprised to see us; luckily, it came up short of the big roll, fishtailing out of sight with a middle finger taking up space in the rear window.

So far, two near misses. With the third time being the charm playing through my wig, I started down the first two hundred and circled the car lot without a problem. Had to stop and let a pack get by, and then started back up the last two hundred. Circled the pumps and put the red and white right in front of the bay. Just as planned. Lit a smoke with a sense of accomplishment and then leaned back.

That's when I caught Stovepipe in the rearview mirror again. It was the second time he spoke since the gas pumps. He saw we were lined up with the bay and caught my eyes in the mirror, then dropped, "Perfect."

The whole scene left me feeling like I had soloed during the near miss with the New Yorker and 'operation figure eight.' The whole episode up to that point was like some condensed microcosm of a larger experience. Like a war, where I carried out the struggle, and Pipe was like the government, doing little and allowing the whole thing to unfold for some strange and unknown reason.

There are times when I think about that figure eight and wonder if the Pipe was really in the back seat. Sometimes, I see him coming out of the john right after the eight was made. Seeing how things were lining up, and then dropping the "perfect" on me. Sometimes, I think I was the only one riding the Comet, just don't know.

******

Up to this point, everything that had happened was just a preliminary bout before the main event. Somehow, Pipe convinced me it would be a good idea to take it to the next level and put the 63 in the bay, maybe even on the rack, and go to work.

And looking back, it wasn't any different than one country invading another; that's the level I should have caught, but it blew by me like a fastball as Pipe kept putting down what a good idea the approach was, his head rhythmically moving up and down with each word that came out of it.

Up to then, I'd always respected Ernie's space. I did gas and windshields, radiators, and dipsticks. I didn't mess with the nerve center of the station. If I did anything in that bay, it was to pass through it to get to the candy machine, like some cowboy traveling through Indian Territory, Ernie's eyes on me every step of the way. Hell, his buddy, Ed, who saved his life in Korea, wasn't allowed to pick up a stinking tool in that bay.

But Pipe kept pitching, "Catch this place. Dig! The layout! You got everything you need to get the gear I'm missing." I started to buy into his rap that ninety percent of Ernie was how he had the place laid out and having the right tools to make the motors sound like fine-tuned instruments, and ten percent experience and knowledge. I know now, and I actually knew back then Pipe had the percentages backwards, but at the time, in a bizarre way, it was all making perfect sense.

The Comet was lined up perfectly for the rack as I gazed at it from inside the bay. All I had to do was lift the door and, back it in and go to work. Catching the workbench and the rack, the lighting with every tool in view, the calendar with some gorgeous chick in some provocative pose, it all started to roll like the evening tide coming in with no way to stop.

Went to the grease rack and then to the wall that held the controls, read the labels, and played with the levers. After a few minutes, I felt I could raise the Comet. Next, I raised the garage door that went up with little effort, just what you would expect from something that had been well-maintained. Got in the 63, turned her over, and backed her onto the rack. Gaining more and more confidence every step of the way that I knew what I was doing.

Got out, gazed at her, and then began to think of the uncharted waters I was about to enter and in whose domain. If ever the time had come to second-guess the situation, it was at this point. Pipe caught the momentary hesitation and, without a word, got in the back seat and looked up like one looks up to heaven to invoke some divine will. After a short wait, he then raised his right arm and pointed in the same direction. Next thing I know I'm working the levers to the rack and walking under the belly of the Comet, having never gone this far before.

I barked my first command in Ernie's bay, telling Pipe, "Turn her over." Pipe leaned over the back of the front seat and flipped the keys. The motor caught on about the fifth try, and I began to examine her belly. I couldn't catch anything specific, except all the brake lines, and transmission lines vibrated like hell.

I barked my second order, "Give her some gas." This command put the Pipe out, and I heard him mutter a long, drawn-out "Man" as he wrestled his way from the back seat to the front and behind the steering wheel. The 63 gave both of us quite a start as the movement from front to back seat caused her to shift a little on the rack.

After the shift, I gave Pipe the signal, and he tromped down on the gas; within seconds, hot transmission fluid streamed from a line, just missing my face but hitting my chest. I yelled at him to, "Back off!" And then informed him I'd caught the problem, as I wiped the fluid not off my shirt, but into it.

It was a nice shirt—one of my better ones for work—but the fact that it was ruined was secondary to how the puzzle of the missing gear was starting to come together. Learned the 63 was losing fluid under pressure. All you had to do was stop the leak and put the fluid back. And a feeling came over me that the Pipe was right, I was a mechanic, and all I really needed was the right time, place, and tools to let it all come together.

Like the shirt, the fact that I was in Ernie's holy land and that he could show up at any given moment was completely beyond my comprehension. I felt in control of the situation, and if anything, I was becoming Ernie.

As I made my way to my car to get a sweatshirt that had been living in my back seat for a couple of months to replace the shirt I had just ruined, how I would attack the problem linecame to me as I lit a smoke. I felt like a prizefighter moving to my corner after the third round, knowing I had the fight and that my opponent had nothing. I could walk through anything he had. Then, I got myself a Coke as a reward before coming off the stool and answering the bell.

It was perfect as I drank and smoked in the forbidden bay, anxious to start the next round. I spent some time just looking at Ernie's workbench. It looked like some aisle in a hardware store. And I knew whatever I needed to get the Pipe rolling wasprobably on or in that bench somewhere, and it was just a matter of time before I found it.

The search turned up some small I.D hydraulic hose, a ton of small screw clamps, along with a hacksaw instead of a tube cutter because, at the time, I had no idea what a tube cutter was. I butted my smoke, put down my Coke, and then put about fivepieces of gum in my mouth. The plan was simple: cut out the bad part, temporarily plug one end of the line with the gum, get the hose over the other end, clamp it, remove the gum, put the hose over that end, and clamp it. Bingo! And so I went to work.

Somewhere into the line I was operating on, it started - the payoff. Right above me came the tunes, caught the loud click that fired up the reel-to-reel, and Stovepipe took the volume up to some perfect level to get the best sound. The sounds were beyond Elvis or Chuck Berry, Ray Charles or Buddy Holly, Johnny Cash or Marvin Gaye, B.B. King or Eric Clapton, andthe entire fine licks other cats like them ever put out.

Like all the good licks have their origin from above and have been played just once before, the great are the ones who've heard from the cat right over my head working the Wollensak. The best sound from the infant interstate highway system, when Fords and Chevys were the most common ride on their back, as they began to wind through the countryside, cutting down the time at red lights. The time when the radio took a back seat to the TV at home but got the front seat in the car, the time of 'mobile music.' You didn't have to stay at home anymore to catch the tunes.

No two ways about it. I was getting high, high on life, or the secondhand smoke coming from the back seat overhead. The tunes let me move through my work like I had two brains, one that controlled my movements and the other that controlled my thoughts. My hands knew what to do, and that freed up my wig to let me go wherever the tunes took me.

So it wasn't a surprise, but more like a pleasant rush when Mr. Gilbert, my eighth-grade American history teacher, started handing me tools; for some reason, the second brain invited him there. And all he could talk about was Detroit - "Straight Detroit," to be exact, back when Antoine de Lamothe Cadillac put the French stamp on the terrain about 1701.

The "straight" threw me, and for a moment, I figured Mr. Cadillac picked up the village of Detroit in some card game. But Mr. Gilbert put me right by putting on me "Detroit" means "straight," referring to the twenty-seven-mile river that ran by the village. Detroit was what the settlers called the river, and that's how it ran – straight.

Then he told me Detroit is the only point on the international boundary between the U.S. and Canada where Canada lies directly south of U.S. territory. That back in Cadillac's day, the biggest float for your boat on the Great Lakes was from Buffalo to Detroit; it was the farthest point west for a long time. It was the only big town out west and made it a whole "c" note before Chicago even thought about showing up.

The music coming from above started to catch every beat of the manufacturing that went on not only in Detroit as the years rolled by but all over the country during the time when everyone was just starting to catch their breath after the "second big one"- the beginning of the "Boom."

Seems everyone was glad to see everyone after the "second big one." It got pretty friendly, and the population was starting to show it - the time when me and all the cats I know made the big slide. And just as fast as Mr. Gilbert appeared, he disappeared.

But it wasn't too long after Mr. Gilbert, as the tunes just kept rolling on, that Carmen Basilio and Sugar Ray Robinson started working the tools. Both were lost in some conversation that concerned Bob Cousy of the Celtics and Jim Brown of the Cleveland Browns. Each taking some position that was beyond me, a conversation I only caught part of, seems I came in the middle of something about hand and foot speed.

I kept working, but it was like I wasn't there, and it seemed that their conversation was like their fights on the Gillette Cavalcade of Sports, neither one giving an inch on the position each had taken on which type of speed was the better procession using Cousy and Brown as examples.

The illusion of both of them evolved into a memory of being

home on some hot, late August night, watching the two fight. My dad always tuned in to the fights. Sugar Ray came out of Detroit, and Basilio was from New England, and when they started to cook it was all about talent and heart, all part of boxing back then, all part of the "Big Boom."

When the fights came on, my mom would leave the room in mild protest over the brutality of the sport. She'd try to take me with her, but my dad would start talking to me, and I'd get to stay. "This is what the two do for a job; this is what they work at; boxers of their caliber are damn good, and so is the money they're earning."

It was a statement of legitimacy directed more at Mom than me; at that time, I didn't have any idea what 'caliber' meant, but he was letting her know that sometimes brutality is what brings talent and heart to the surface. To be seen, understood, and appreciated. That in the most general of terms, there is no good without some bad. That fighting for a belt or what you want isn't wrong.

The tunes kept up at a consistent pace surrounding me, and for the only time in my life, I saw what I was hearing. My hands knew what to do, and I started to throw the parts together in nice combinations - both fighters complementing me on my hand and foot speed.

And as my hands and feet moved, I found myself going back to the municipal swimming pool, and the big-tire Schwinn that got me there thought of and saw cats I hadn't seen in years. All kinds of situations and cats blowing through my wig, dormant memories and new thoughts kept popping me left and right, out of nowhere, with a lot of power behind them.

Then, my hands stopped, and for a moment I panicked. For a brief moment, I stood under the 63 with a cast characters, wondering what was going to happen next. All who visited me standing in their own space and time, just looking at me, and me looking at them. Each disappearing in their own way, yet the tunes kept playing, and there seemed to be no apparent reason for them to leave - except for one. The job was finished.

It was time for the decision. I had taken it as far as I could under the Comet. There was nothing left to do other than to see if the effort would make the red and white move.

Lowered the rack, replaced the lost fluid, and got in the Comet, the tunes still playing. Never checked the mirror to see what the Pipe was doing, lost in the anticipation, if the referee would raise my arm in victory.

Got the 63 off the rack, and everything held; hit the gas and drove it off. I didn't have to push it. There have been only a few times since that I've had such a feeling of accomplishment. It was real close to sex, fixing that ride.

Wiped down the crime scene and, like Pipe's *Bagpipes and Bongos,* felt I pulled it off. The Pipe was rolling again, and Ernie wouldn't be any the wiser on how the whole thing came down. Or at least that's what I thought.

I had to think that way because Ernie was also known down at the V.F.W and a few local bars as "Yalu Ernie." He'd done both sides of the 38th parallel in Korea. Made it all the way up to the Yalu River and back again, with the 1st Cav. The same patch I wore eighteen years later in Tay Ninh Province. Ernie hired me because we wore the same patch when no one was that interested in hiring me because of where I'd been.

He was basically a great guy, but when you flipped certain switches, he could turn himself into another person. The kind of person who could flip out Jack the Ripper or CharlesManson, guys like them. One of those switches being where hemade his living, the bay, the line I just crossed, and the holy land I just invaded.

This was the last thought that popped into my wig as the Pipe emerged from the back seat. In celebration, we burned one during a short test drive that seemed like it took five hours but was really five minutes. We parked the 63 next to the 66' Biscayne and caught the end of the tapes.

******

The trip around the block, that seemed like a good idea, eventually turned out to be a bad idea, and the buzz went negative about ten minutes after Ernie got back to the station and found it unattended. That's about the time it took him to notice the Comet next to the Biscayne, with Pipe and me dazedby all the tunes heard, pretty much oblivious to everything except what was playing in our minds.

The mood was shattered as a big hammy fist began to pound on the passenger window, my window, with a threatening voice asking, "What the hell you think you're doing?" And it might have sounded like a question, but it wasreally a command to come up with the right answer or face theconsequences. In view of the trip around the block, I knew coming up with the right answer had a real low probability.

So, it became one of those paradoxes of life. I sure wasn't going to tell old "Yalu" that for the last two or three hours, I was hanging out in his bay putting the Comet I was sitting in, that was now running and running good, back together. No, I had to go with the standard, "Nothing." Had to give him a false admission that I was goofing off when actually I was workingand take the heat.

Pipe and Ernie hardly paid attention to each other. Other cats had stopped by enough that Ernie took the Pipe to be another one of my goofy buddies. He was after me, for sure, allthe way. For all he cared, Pipe could hang around if he wantedto witness something really gruesome.

There was no two ways about it. Ernie was agitated, and when I learned the cause of his agitation, a real short but heavy- duty panic ran through me like a runaway freight train. "You know, while you and your buddy here were goofing off in this piece of shit – somebody was in my shop!" The tone and expression leading to a very simple conclusion that whoever that somebody was, their next stop would be intensive care.

Ernie herded Pipe and me to the bay like a couple of calveshe'd pulled from a briar patch. A mushroom cloud popped intomy mind as I envisioned our arrival at the bay, and for the second time in one day, I saw my life flash in front of me. Wondering what the giveaway was. What did I forget in the wipe-down? What did I forget to put away? The answer Erniegave me being the last thing I heard in my short life.

Turned out it was the hacksaw that was the only thing Erniehad. But it was large. There it was, right under the calendar where I left it, as opposed to by the candy machine where I gotit. And I felt the big confession coming on like a fast horse in the Kentucky Derby. My world was about to end. I accepted this, but not Pipe.

It was clear I moved from employee to suspect. Sure enough, Ernie wasn't shy about pointing out, over and over again, that the saw was over by the candy machine next to the half-eaten bag of peanuts when he'd left. "How the hell did it get under the calendar?" The only explanation being somebody moved it, meaning some unauthorized person was in the bay and that someone was going to pay in spades.

I was just at the point of giving Ernie the full confession he wanted when the Stovepipe broke into the investigation. In a play only the Pipe could pull off, he got Ernie's and my attention from the hacksaw to the calendar it was under. He directed our eyes to the woman and then, as smooth as a shot of top-shelf whiskey murmured, "Miss America, 1950." Once he had our attention, he moved through the bay telling us all he knew about Miss America 1950.

This stopped Ernie right in his tracks. Ernie put his two good eyes on Pipe's one and, like a junkyard dog, barked, "What!" Pipe rolled on and gave Ernie her name, measurements, what state she was from, what she wanted to be, and so on. Ernie let him roll on, too, nodding his head up and down with a maniacal smile that left you unsure of how he was taking all of this. But one thing was for sure: we'd move from the hacksaw and how it got over to the calendar to what seemed to be an even more important topic. One that held Ernie.

The whole time this was going on, Pipe had moved from the candy machine to the calendar, holding our attention by what he was putting down; his movement went more or less unnoticed. Finally, Ernie called his bluff, and this was when I learned there was no Miss America 1950. Ernie tells Pipe, "You're full of shit."

No, it's true. Later on, I checked the almanac, and she's not there. Why? Who knows, that never came up in the forty-five minutes of being the butt of Ernie's jokes once Pipe admitted that Ernie was right. Me, not Pipe.

I can still see Ernie looking at me and saying, "You've brought a lot of dimwits around this station, but this guy takes the cake. Miss America 1950!" And that was the beauty of the Pipe at that moment; he was willing to let Ernie be the world's smartest guy while he played the world's dumbest.

I can also still see the Pipe placing the hacksaw next to the half a bag of peanuts by the candy machine as he made his exit. In my book, he won the Academy Award for the character he played in the bay. Ernie followed Pipe right to his car, on him all the way about Miss America 1950, enjoying every minute of it, Pipe leaving him with the final word on Miss America 1950. "Dig! She was my mom." And to this day, I don't know where I'm at with that, but I wouldn't be surprised. Later on, Ernie told me the reason there was no Miss America 1950 was because Mary Catherine Campell, from Ohio, won the Miss America Pageant twice, once in 1922 and again in 1923. Ernie believed 1950 was the year they adjusted for Ohio's two-time winner. One of several explanations out there as to why there was no Miss America 1950.

I felt helpless when I followed them to the '63, afraid to say anything out of fear we might return to an earlier subject. But after a while, that feeling just came and went as we headed back to the bay, and the saw was where it was supposed to be, where it had been left by Ernie, and I let Ernie know that as far as I was concerned the idea that someone was in his bay was the product of his overworked imagination.

How'd Pipe come up with Miss America 1950, who knows? That was the Stovepipe. That's why he always bubbled to the top when the cats that knew him started to rap. And that's pretty much *Atomic Peanut* in a nutshell; know where the name comes from, heard the tunes, and most of all, know what it accomplished. It's all talent and heart.

Pipe gave me the album that day. He pulled it from a box he had in the trunk. The jacket cover had a black background with an exploding white peanut under a gray mushroom cloud. I didn't have it long. Told Ernie how great it was and let him borrow it, and he returned only part of it. He and his girlfriend had a fight one night, and along with the vases, clocks, and pictures that got smashed was this precious album. I should have known better. They had a history of not breaking up but of breaking things. Now, all I have is part of the album.

The 63 Comet was the last car I got moving from my own efforts. What I accomplished that day I took in other directions. I worked for Ernie right until he died - about six months later. After he got sick and I'd visit him, he'd always apologize about the album and ask, "That Miss America guy – what's he doing these days?" I'd always answer, "Wish I knew. I never caught him again." We'd both smile and then he'd close his eyes.

Eventually heard somewhere along the line that Stovepipe blew out overweight on a bus, probably because his Comet had burned out down the road at some station that didn't have a mechanic.

Album 4: Radio Ventriloquist (According to Dart

Around 1970, I was putting the finishing touches on three days I'd pulled down at the Fairfield County Jail in Ohio for having an open container in a moving vehicle. I was sitting on the top of the fourth floor of an ancient municipal building, waiting out one more day and night before I could go downstairs and get out of there. During that time, I bumped into two Stovepipes. Stove Pipe and Stovepipe, just when one left, the other arrived.

At the time, it was just me and maybe six other guys sharing six bunks, two picnic tables, and one circular barred window that looked down on the streets of Lancaster in what was referred to as a "dormitory setting" for society's less- threatening criminals. The occupants came and went at a rate that there was always plenty of room for additional violators of the Ohio Revised Code, such as the Pipe.

Prior to that, it had been a rough two days, starting with me blowing south down Route 33, popping the top off a Blatz to take the edge off—doing about seventy downhills with a strong tailwind.

From the start, it was hardly a fair contest, me in a six- cylinder push-button Dart and an Ohio Bear on top of an eight billion cubic inch Plymouth Fury coming down on me out of nowhere like a rocket.

I picked him up in my rearview mirror, and in the blink of an eye, we were side by side just as I brought the beer to the top of the wheel. And if timing is everything, it was good for him and bad for me. It was as if I couldn't stop myself as I pulled the top off like I was pulling the pin on a hand grenade as we exchanged glances. It happened that fast, he caught me with both hands-on top of the wheel, working the can. He knewwhat I was doing. He had me, and I could see it in his eyes.

Probably, it was the extra mile and a half I dragged him down the road while trying to figure out what to do with the newly-opened brew that pissed him off. However, I did pull over as soon as he turned the siren on. Yup - got me right undera billboard that read, "Keep America Beautiful – Get a Haircut."

I figured I'd just get a ticket, be told to get a haircut, the standard lecture, and then be on my way. That's what I thoughtas I lit a smoke and waited for him to make it up to the open driver-side window.

He filled the side view mirror. One hand had a thumb tucked in a belt loop by his gun, the other held his hat. He wore a starched, black, short-sleeve shirt, three gold rockers on each sleeve, a big gold badge pinned over the left pocket, and gray pants with one yellow stripe running down the outside of each leg. The "Badge" looked like trouble.

But I was feeling okay with everything; getting my wallet out it was going to cost me a little time and a little money, andthat would probably be it. Two commodities I was short on, but I could get through this. I was all right. I never took a hit from the can; there was nothing on my breath.

But late morning, that beautiful summer day was to be filled with surprises, none of which would be good. The first one being informed that not only did I have an open container in a moving vehicle in excess of the posted speed limit, I was moving said open container and exceeding the speed limit on an expired license.

Actually, the conversation was pretty short; there weren't any of the standard questions, like, "Do you know how fast you were going?" Or "Is that an open beer in your vehicle?" No, allI got were a set of instructions to follow him to the county seat, and it snowballed from there.

And where I thought the situation would be confined to a cop and a ticket, it actually escalated to a judge and a courtroom. A courtroom half filled with knuckleheads such asme, all in violation of some statute of the Ohio Revised Code.I'd been to traffic court before, and the odds of coming out unscathed were about the same as getting hit by a meteor. So Iknew there would be some pain, I just didn't know how much.

The judge was true to form, a man of few words and little compassion, the compassion dwindling more and more with each person that stood before him as the late morning turned to early afternoon and then late afternoon.

As I waited my turn, I began to plan my defense, which in the end didn't really take that long, having been caught red- handed. So, rather than a defense, I mulled over in my mind the best way to throw myself at the mercy of the court. To come up with the perfect explanation of why opening a beer in a moving vehicle while driving on an expired license, supposedly ten miles over the speed limit, seemed like a goodidea.

And try as I would, I couldn't come up with an equation that would balance the problem. This became a problem in itself because I noticed as the afternoon wore on the sentences were getting a little stiffer with each lame story the black robeheard.

But, on the other hand, I was looking pretty clean for my day in court; hair might have been a touch too long, themustache didn't help, but I had on a nice shirt and a good pairof jeans compared to the competition. Unlike some of the others who went in front of me, I could string a sentence together and do an act of contrition.

I began to believe that the situation I faced would be a good benchmark of the university training I'd received over the pasttwo years; that an educated person would be able to get out from under something like this.

I liked my chances of getting out of there. I felt I could beatthe weekend in jail the previous two guys received, eventhough their infractions were on a lower level compared to mine. I had to take that approach.

Looking back, when my turn finally came, I felt I handled myself pretty good, right up to the point where the judge askedwhat I did, and I told him that I was a student.

That was a huge tactical error at the time because, at that particular time in history, students were pretty much burning down or tearing up just about anything they got around. To thisday, I believe if I'd said something more like I was planning tobecome a student, working in some innuendo regarding the GI Bill and the time I'd served, I'd have walked. But that wasn't the case. Back then, you didn't bring it up.

First, the apprehending officer surprised me with his clocking and had me doing eighty in a sixty. Then, the judge really surprised me with his $150 fine or three days in jail. This after he acquainted me with the number of traffic fatalities, in just his jurisdiction, let alone Ohio, caused by people who'd been drinking and driving.

He ended by letting me know, "It's coming to an end. Courts are clamping down. Tell your friends."

I thought about it for a moment. I'd been back two years, but before I left, no one went anywhere without a six-pack in the car. It didn't change for me when I got back. It wasn't a bigdeal.

But the judge was right; since I'd been home, I did have some friends who'd told me about getting beat up in court for what I faced. That it was turning into a big deal. But that was them, not me. However, the way things were shaping up, it was starting to seem I'd be just like them. I'd be finding out first hand and probably be passing on the court's message, just likethem.

He didn't leave me much to work with, the situation comingdown to my near-empty wallet and my skill to negotiate. So I started from the position that I could do about a quarter of the fine then and there and get the rest to the court by the end of the week, explaining the 'rest' was in Columbus. But my goal was to fork over the quarter and get the judge the rest. If he accepted the partial payment but didn't drop the balance, and I got to go get the rest, Lancaster would just become a town to avoid in my future travels.

I had to set some targets and goals as I went forward and had to have someplace where I wanted to be if I was to put in the all-out effort. The whole time, trying to avoid what was fast, becoming apparent that there wasn't much of a fuse left on the black robe.

I presented the judge a plan and drew upon every presentation skill I'd learned in school the past two years: good posture, minimum movement, proper grammar, and a fair tone of speech. Pointing out that although I did open the beer in a moving vehicle, I never consumed any of it. Spent a fair amount of time telling the judge what a good risk I was, confidently ending that I could fulfill any obligation given to me by the court if just given a chance and a little time to makethings right.

In fact, the longer I talked, the better I felt. Through it all, I maintained pretty good eye contact. Only time the contact was broken was when the judge would take a pull from an oversized coffee mug.

With each pull came a complementary wince, and you could tell the brew that was hitting his pit was at room temperature, a little bitter and full of acid. This didn't stop him; seems he, too, was suffering from an addiction.

The way he moved after each pull gave up the fact that he was uncomfortable. That a Rolaids about the size of a manhole cover would be needed to soak up what was fast looking for the backdoor. I blamed that coffee mug for what followed.

The judge took little time and spoke to me in a pleasant manner when I had finished; his words at the end, along the lines that he didn't see any risk either, followed by a friendly smile.

Then, there was a short pause to allow me to savor his remark and for him to visit the bathroom. And for a brief moment, I felt that I'd pulled it off, and in that moment, it appeared I would be getting better than expected for my efforts. Needless to say, I was a little surprised; especially with the fact that maybe I had learned a few things from my academic endeavors over the past two years.

It was wishful thinking on my part. When the judge returned, he presented in more detail the view of the court as far as risk was concerned, which in turn hinged on one simplequestion that was to be answered with either a "yes" or a "no."Simply put, could I pay the fine in full today? I got hit with a question so easy and, at the same time, so hard to answer.

As I pondered my reply, the judge continued with the view of the court by pointing out that I'd already demonstrated what kind of a risk I was by opening a beer in a moving vehicle, doing eighty in a sixty, and driving on an expired license. And that if I'd been paying attention, the gentleman before me who had all but ten dollars of his fine went "upstairs," and that I would be spending the weekend with him, that I'd wasted some of the court's time, and now the court was going to waste a little of mine. It was a real lesson in civics.

******

They took me upstairs after I turned in my wallet, belt, and shoelaces. Naturally, I'd just missed dinner, and based on the guys I'd be spending the weekend with, it was more of a blessing than a curse. If there is one thing, I'll always remember about that weekend hiatus, it's the food.

The prison population was a mixed bag of white, black, and Hispanic guys, oldest guy maybe thirty. Most were doing time for moving violations, like me, some disorderly conduct, and two guys who pulled down the most time were in for indecent exposure.

There was a marathon game of euchre at one picnic table and a gin game at another. Given their crimes, the way they looked, and how they talked, I was kind of embarrassed by the fact that I didn't see any problem fitting right in. Talked in passing to everyone, and by midnight, the guilt of what I'd done that day and whose company I was in was not enough to keep me from sleeping rather soundly.

Next morning, I woke up for breakfast—a large scoop of oatmeal in a melmac bowl and a pint of whole white milk at room temperature. Next to the bowl, on an oversized tray that made all the objects on it look small, was a piece of unbuttered white toast. No condiments. The only extras were the plastic spoon and napkin. It was a rough start for a guy who hates oatmeal.

About mid-morning, a cat blew in from downstairs, a little different than the rest of us. He was in for a one-nighter in transit to Cleveland; apparently, someone downstairs wanted to rap with him before he got a little too far north and lost in the system. He was an Ohio boy caught in Kentucky, did something big, wearing a patch over one eye.

He didn't catch my attention until he started telling everyone that he went by "Stove Pipe." He made a big deal of how it was two words, not one. The way he said it made you think "Stove" was his first name and "Pipe" his last. Put down, he was this big-time musician that sat in with all the popular area bands. As soon as this came out, I watched him real close because I had some buddies that couldn't stop rapping about some cat they called Stovepipe.

I'd heard all about *Save Your Strength, Bagpipes, and Bongo's,* not to mention *Atomic Peanut,* to the point where I felt I was there with the cats that caught it firsthand. What they put down was heavy duty because the cats that put me on to Stovepipe didn't even catch Pipe firsthand. They just knew some cat that knew some cat, if you know what I mean.

Eventually, I got into a mainstay full-blown rap with Stove Pipe just around lunchtime. And what I thought was a little off center, as I forced down a sandwich—two pieces of bread and a piece of baloney—followed by an apple that had more bruises than a stepchild, a carrot that had been pulled from the ground at the turn of the century, room temperature whole white milk, and no condiments, was that he was more interested in what I knew about him than in being Stovepipe if you catch my drift.

He couldn't tell me any more about, say, *Atomic Peanut* or *Bagpipes and Bongo's* than some of the cats I ran with, yet he was supposed to be the cat that put them out there.

This cat didn't have any physical presence, he was awkward, and he wasn't the fastest gun in the West when it came to unloading his wig. He certainly wasn't holding the cards everyone seemed to think he had.

In fact, at one point, he told me his daddy was the Duke of Pedecah, and that certainly wasn't what I'd heard. The more we talked, the more I couldn't wait to get back and tell my buddies how lame Stovepipe was. What note on the patch? He couldn't even follow that. It was like he wanted to take notes on all I was putting down instead of the other way around.

Pretty tough critique, but what cemented the deal that he probably was the Pipe was that during his weakening performance, he produced a picture of Verne and Ida, Greyhound bus station and all. He pulled it from his shirt pocket like you pull out a pack of smokes, which in turn would be like the last thing he'd pull from his shirt pocket, the way he started bumming smokes the moment he arrived.

This was one topic he was well versed on had all the background, and anybody who knows anything about Stovepipe knows about Verne and Ida. He'd been around some cats. The whole thing came down as a huge disappointment as I watch him feebly light the second smoke, he bummed from me while he went on about the two.

No, this couldn't be the cat that was out there, that every other cat was starting to dig. That some said when he put downa lick or laid down a rap for the first time, the right big-time tune-maker somewhere out there in the world would catch, nomatter where, no matter what – other side of the planet. No, this cat's influence was, at best anemic. But, then again, he hadthe proof, he had the picture, and he was strong on that part; itwas rough, double rough.

And it finally came down from the turn-key to one of the inmates who passed it on that Stove Pipe was popped for stealing and dealing in high-end hot tractors: Kentucky, Indiana, Pennsylvania, Ohio, didn't matter. And he followed Stovepipe from band to band in his free time. What he had going was he looked like Stovepipe's twin brother and had been confused for the real Pipe on more than one occasion. He told the cops more than once it couldn't have been him; he was playing a gig, and when they checked it and showed his picture to the bar owners, they always covered him, except for one time. It took a while to catch him, but they finally caught on. Oh! I had a lot to drop on everyone once I got out, and I brokeoff the rap and took my contempt over to my bunk and slept right through dinner and into the mid-afternoon of the next day.

******

When I came out of my sleep, Stove Pipe was gone, and I began to tune in this new cat on the floor that the magistrate had just sent upstairs. Apparently, they ran the downstairs seven days, the judge doing five, and the magistrate the weekends. This new cat was flapping right and left about this "defendant" he'd just caught downstairs.

"Pretty soon, they're going to bring up the boy that put the ace lick on the black robe and all his pals downstairs." No two ways about it: whatever went down impressed this cat, and he became like John the Baptist for the one who was soon to be with us.

It was all about this cat and his Comet blowing down 33 over eighty miles an hour. It seemed they liked the number 'eighty' in that county seat. Anyway, the cat went on like he was directly quoting from the official court record: the robe said this, the cat said that, and so on. Gigging it to the point where the cat let the robe know fifty-five cents out of the Comet while riding the snake, in his world, would be like breaking the sound barrier. It couldn't push eighty, even if it wanted to. The Comet became evidence, exhibit A.

The new cat went on, "This boy is as smooth as top-shelf whiskey." Talked about how he offered the robe his keys. "Catch it for yourself, get eighty out of her; she's yours, that ride loves me, but she can't give me eighty, won't give you eighty either, and that's a cold hard fact."

The new cat on the floor rolled on, there was no doubt about it, and those who were there will tell you the defendant had everyone in the courtroom in his pocket. To them, it seemed a fair offer. But the real cold hard fact was that the robe didn't have to take the Comet for a ride and didn't care about his pockets.

In comparison, he put on the defendant he had the track record of the arresting officer and, more importantly, the "power" of the court to determine guilt or innocence. After this told the defendant he was going to be incarcerated. The defendant didn't blink and put on the magistrate how he felt about this "power," pointing out he wasn't feeling the scales of justice in the robe's court. Told the robe he'd seen better kangaroos at the zoo. He wasn't afraid to step over the line.

The cat, putting on the rap about the gig downstairs, began to directly quote what happened next and footnoted that fact as he began on how the defendant closed. "I don't look like you, think like you, or act like you. I don't put a strain on you. I didn't come looking for you; you came looking for me to show me what you got because I'm not like you or your boy."

At this point, the cat mentioned how the defendant stopped and gazed at the badge that had pulled him in. He explained how he eyeballed the uniform up and down for just the right amount of time and with just the right expression to make his point before he picked it up again. He got him to blink.

"I didn't do anything to put me in front of you. Just because you have the juice to put me where you want don't make it right; that's something we both know, don't we? You're not going to be upfront, you're going to do what you want. And that's the name of that tune, so go ahead and play it."

The opening act rolled on to the point where neither I nor the other cats caught the entrance of the cat from downstairs, the "defendant." It was like he just materialized out of nowhere by a vacant bunk, acknowledging everyone with a nod.

Next, he walked to the picnic table closest to the window, threw down a fresh pack of smokes, sat down, opened the pack, took one, and then threw the pack back on the table. He got some pats on the back, some handshakes, and when things cooled down, told everyone he was Stovepipe and then added, "That's one word - not two."

I never left the bunk. I wanted to, but for some reason couldn't move. I returned his nod, and that was about it. I caught his patch and the musical note on it, the tri-color white, gray, and black of what he was wearing, and the concern he had about his red and white 63 Comet, now also in custody. From everything I'd caught from the cats I ran with, he was definitely hitting the profile.

And where the Pipe from the other night had the picture of Verne and Ida, this cat had the red and white 63 mentioned more than once by any cat that knew anything about Stovepipe.

No problem, when you really thought about it - coming up with a picture of a couple of midgets in front of a bus station. But coming up with a red and white 63 Comet, well, that was the trump card. There just weren't that many of them around, and the ones that were around, a normal person wouldn't want to drive, except for a cat like the Pipe.

It was all falling together. And what really hit me was the fact that the cat at the picnic table, smoking and joking with the convicts, was a cat that other cats were now beginning to imitate, and after about a half hour of being around him, you could see why he was fluid. He was coming across just as advertised.

I wanted to break the whole tale down to the Pipe about the cat from the night before. But by the time I made the table, the Pipe had produced a shirt pocket-sized transistor radio and placed it next to the pack of smokes, changing everything.

From that point on, the cat from the other night never came up by me or by anyone. I've often wondered why. After the "shirt pocket" hit the table, the imposter was forgotten. It was strange because you'd have thought it would've been the first topic to come up, but it never surfaced.

The topic pretty much turned to how Stovepipe got the radio on the floor in the first place. All Pipe put down, "They got everything below the belt. I got everything above it." Then he began a rap about some station he wanted to catch around midnight.

Actually, it wasn't a station at all, but some airwave pirates, sailing their ship, a big transmitter, under a flag that had no paperwork behind it and no call letters on it. Pipe then putting down, "Sometimes you have to fly under the radar to catch what you want. Dig! Underground radio!"

Even though no one knew what he was talking about, a chorus rose up from the ranks in smooth-voiced agreement, everyone pretending they listen to the underground radio all the time.

It was more than a couple hours before midnight when Stovepipe put on us what the schedule would be, firmly pointing out that whatever the rap, and no matter where it was, it ended at midnight, and then he kicked it off about the "three" sides to every coin. After the kickoff, the hours we had before midnight blew by like minutes.

Stovepipe gazed the environment gave a short sigh, the kind of sigh that you couldn't tell if it was one of anxiety or relief. It was a sigh that understood the surroundings – jail – which gave it an anxious tone. But then that tone was offset by the relieving tone of found time. The two offsetting tones blended into an interesting melody.

The time and place to put down some loose change that had been rattling around in the pockets of his wig for some time. The "three-sided coin" everyone forgets the edge.

After the sigh, everyone reached for a smoke at once, taking advantage of the open pack on the table, and each began to settle in and around the table. Everyone but Pipe stood by the window, and he smoked when he noticed no one else was smoking. And where it seemed the smoke burned fast, when Pipe fired up a smoke, it seemed to last forever. The boy couldnurse a smoke.

And an unspoken rule developed that when Pipe smoked, no one else smoked and vise-versa. Looking back, it was kind of mystical; that pack among all us seemed to last most of the night, yet at the same time, from the moment the sigh ended, there was always a smoke burning. The whole scene always reminded me of some miniature nicotine Sermon on the Mount.

Stovepipe began in so many words, "Us cats and kitties always buy into the two sides of everything." Then he went down the list. "The platter has its A side, B side, we got men and women, black and white, old and young, war and peace, Fords and Chevy's, National League and American League, Democrats and Republicans, liberals, and conservatives – you name it. Well, they're all coins in our pockets that we take outan occasionally flip to make a hard decision easy."

Pipe went on to explain how when a coin goes into the air and when it lands how, we expect one side or the other. Everycat looks at two possible outcomes when there are actually three. The one in a billionth time the coin lands on its edge. "See, we forget the edge, but that doesn't mean it can't happen; it's a possible outcome, it's just that it hardly ever happens, butit can happen, and you can't rule it out."

The time began to roll by as he got deeper into the anatomy of the coin and its three sides. Pointing out that what separates heads from tails is the middle, and what holds the middle is the edge, the third side. And eventually, Pipe produced a coin for all of us to stick in our wig, and it had two sides, rich and poor, thick and thin.

He rapped on how the middle separates the two, to the point where you didn't have to be a rocket scientist to pick up that he was getting into society and its classes, ending with the fact that the middle that separates the two sides was common to all societies on the planet, and when it gets squeezed and thinned out, that's when the problems start. "It's all about thick and thin," Pipe put down as he reached for a smoke. He footnoted after he lit it, "Want a coin with the big edge, thick middle, a third side with the edge of a tire, a big middle class separating rich and poor."

The setting was perfect as I look back. A few cats at the table, a few more hanging by the nearby bunks, mentally scarfing up what Stovepipe was putting down. Pipe continued the anatomy of the coin pointing out its political sides; its two surfaces, on one side, the self-righteous right, on the other side, the godless left.

When one side wears down the other, the coin becomes a coin with little in the middle that doesn't spend well. "Rigid or loose." Pipe exhaled. "One side comes up more often than the other in the flip, we become too rigid - 'bout the only thing you're allowed to do is breathe and forget about doing any thinking."

He continued, "Other side shows up more than the other, we become too loose – you can now go beyond breathing right into open sex with animals if you want. Dig! I want the coin with the thick middle and a big edge; the coin that can land straight up where both political sides are standing in view, a coin that can stand on its own because of its thick middle and big edge...a fair coin."

This was all taking place under four dangling light bulbs out of reach above the table. Throwing down the kind of light that if you were an outsider, like the "turn-key," making your rounds, the whole scene presented a kind of subversive look; everyone huddled around one cat, and that cat doing all the talking. Like maybe we were planning the big break.

Next thing we knew, the turnkey was among us running a quick inspection, coupled with the standard threatening remarks. He confiscated one cat's comb to let us know he wasn't playing around but missed the radio. He made us spreadout and then left. As soon as he left, the cat that had the presence of mind to hide the radio, put it back on the table, and we all waited for Stovepipe to pick up where he left off.

At that point, Pipe was on some coin that dealt with crime and punishment. "Dig! What we're catching in this place!" He continued, "Every time we have to deal with the cats downstairs, they deep scratch us for either our time or our money, sometimes both. That's the two sides of that coin, time and money, the two things that most cats have little of, what's missing is the middle – justice. Yeah, justice is becoming the thinnest coin in our pockets."

All the cats were digging the Pipe, including me. But looking back and catching it all with the hind 20/20 vision thatescaped me at the time, fact is every cat in there, including me,got caught doing something. There was no shortage of admissions among the prison population. We were in the rightplace.

And the problem was we thought what we'd done was something minor, while the cats downstairs thought it was something major, and that's the two sides of that coin. And it really came down to what my dad used to always say when I used to tell him how I was actually the victim in the trouble I sometimes got into. After I'd finish, he'd just look at me and tell me, "The prisons are full of innocent people."

I remember Pipe gazed at the clock sitting high at the otherend of the dorm. He sighed, exhaling a cloud of white smoke as if he finally wanted to let it go about the coins in the pocketsof his mind and rest up a bit before he took us all underground.

But that wasn't to be the case; all the cats, including myself, wanted him to press on. Press on about the two sides toeverything and the importance of the middle.

And he half-heartedly picked it up again and started on about the philosophical coin of good and bad and how you don't know which side is going to come up. The cases where bad people have good things happen to them, and good people have bad things happen to them, everyone asks, "Why?" Pipe taking us down the road that good and bad are random events and, most of the time show up when least expected.

He then suddenly stopped, and the next thing heard was a click as he fired up the shirt pocket junior varsity transistor radio just as he'd promised he would when the time was right. And a smooth and unusual voice came from the junior varsity radio lying on the table. "Yeah, I'm your radio ventriloquist," and we all headed underground.

The way he came across, the "RV," for all we knew, could've been Pipe's brother. He made any current and past DJ sound like a kid in comparison, he was light years beyond Wolfman Jack and any cat that wanted to be or act like Jack or any other DJ out there that thought they were news. He was just a shade below Lord Buckley, and he could get your wig rolling with compound interest in what he was putting down. And to this day, what still is really amazing to me is all the convicts heard the RV, while the turn-key didn't seem to hear a thing.

The Radio Ventriloquist started out by explaining how he was working solo that night, rare for a ventriloquist. His sidekick, Art, was out of the trunk and at The United National Equilibrium forum in the southeast, then Art would be heading southwest, then northwest. He'd already done the northeast.

Yeah, they both belonged to the party better known as TUNE and were all about putting more weight in the middle, making the rich less rich and the poor less poor, through protestand song.

He had an easy rhythm, would drop sets of three tunes on the audience, and then grab ten or fifteen cents for himself while giving ninety to eighty-five cents in change for what you caught, leaving you to count your thoughts, happy with the change.

Always painting some background of what went down in the past, what was going down today, and what needed to go down in the future. Then he took it to the edge when explained that the tunes we'd be catching were the work of Stovepipe – one word, not two – his gift to the movement, and Pipe humbly nodded from the window and blew it off like it was nothing.

By this time, the pack of smokes next to the junior varsity radio finally began to thin out, and the ashtrays were getting full. Some really catchy tunes broke out for a moment, a taste of what was to come, and the ashtrays were emptied, and the table filled up again.

Suddenly, out of nowhere, the filtered and unfiltered, regular and menthol surfaced as a pack of Camels, followed by a pack of Luckys, followed by some Marlboros and Winston's, Salems and Kools, hit the table, along with some gum, and a bag of Planters peanuts. Everything that had been held back was out on the table.

And for the next couple hours, the only movement was to the drinking fountain, then the head, and back to the table, not one location on the triangle out of the range of the Radio Ventriloquist.

Not a cat in the place would ever forget where they were sitting, stooping, or standing when they caught: *Every Cat, Myself Included, Where's The Middle*, and *Big Edge* on the underground radio. Not a cat that was there who, like me, probably doesn't try to go back to Fairfield County late spring of every year and catch the tunes again.

Those three cuts alone, along with the others, have caused some major time travel incidents in my life over the years thathave blown me out of the present and back to the past with such velocity and intensity that getting back to the present is somewhere out there in future.

And taking a step back, I can say I've only hit the cage downtown once, but every time I catch one of those tunes blowing through my mind – I'm back in jail and okay with it. Learned some things there.

It was cagey, the RV rapping about the tunes written in Beaufort and played on a sixteen-string fretless guitar. It was the introduction of the "drone strings" to the guitar. Strings that were strung so close to the box that they played off the vibration put through the box by the "straight eight strings." The drone strings were strings that were heard but nevertouched.

That guitar, backed by a keyboard, harp, and small set of drums, was known as the "Acoustical A Bomb." You catch many major fine tune-makers, past and present, coming really close to the sounds heard by us that night, but close is all theycan get.

And a lot of major tune-makers know about the "A bomb," but it's starting to become a fact that only one cat could play it – ask Walsh or Clapton. Only one recording was ever made featuring the A bomb, and I caught it on the underground radio. Who knows what major tune-makers might have caught it alsoand are playing right around the edges of Beaufort and don't even know it.

No one noticed the lights go out, as the "shirt pocket" kept throwing out the sounds. The warm air blowing through the window drove the smoke over our heads down the hall, and allone could catch were the glowing tips of our smokes.

As you came back from either the fountain or the head, thescene looked like fireflies hovering over a picnic table on a nice summer night held in place by the tunes. In fact, it was on one of these sojourns when *Fire Flies and Fire Fights* came on, andit tattooed my wig for good and put a different edge on something I'd experienced but never could explain.

But the A bomb backed perfectly by the other instruments was secondary to the lyrics I caught that night. No two ways about it: it was a sharp protest, pure in nature, bound to open old wounds along with creating some new ones.

The music and lyrics came together like one part oxygen and two parts hydrogen; yeah, it became water that every cat didn't have to drink, but every cat had to taste. It was Guthrie, Seger, Collins, Dylan, Baez, Jagger, Havens, Slick, Lennon, and all the others, all in one voice, putting out the word.

And depending where you were, as far as the "establishment" was concerned, if you were established upstairs around the tables, bunks, and smokes in your early twenties, what came out of the shirt pocket was like a beautiful chick you could take to bed with you at the end of the night andembrace.

If you were established downstairs around the desks, chairs, and paperwork in your late forties, what came out of the pocket was like some nickel/dime diseased whore to be feared andavoided.

And looking back, what came up from the underground thatnight wasn't all right, but it was far from being all wrong. If anything, it was the biggest slice of Americana I've ever had. Everyone got to hear both sides of the record.

If anything, it was a musical compass pointing right at Washington, provoking thoughts about the First Amendment, testing it, playing it right to the edge. Waiting to see what would happen, what direction we were going to take.

Tunes like "Where the Dickens is Marx" still play in my wig like I heard it five minutes ago. And aside from how it rhymed in time and tempo, the music never overtook the lyrics.

The lyrics that defined how the two wrote about the same thing: the human condition. Only Dickens appealed to our empathy, while Marx appealed to our anger. The direction of the tune, if things don't change, empathy evolves to anger andanger, violence.

The irony being the pathology is so well understood, but yet there seems to be no cure for the disease.

The lyrics rhyming and timing the Industrial Revolution, the explosion of production, the demand for raw materials, competition for markets, long-distance trade, improvements in transportation and communications, right into the rural to urban shift, the trade unions, and all the baggage each event left behind.

Overcrowded at work, overcrowded at home, times where the bosses paid with thin coins, keeping the fat ones for themselves, crushing any movement to change like a bug, just part of the landscape that tunes painted.

That night, we must have caught about fifteen cuts with the RV. Wish I could remember them all; they were that tight. I'd know any of them if I ever heard them again.

Two or three have stuck with me over the years, and search as I will and have, I've never caught anything like "Poor Literature," a tune about the realist fiction writers who kept the poor in the public eye.

Cats and books like: Dreiser's *Sister Carrie, Gorky's Lower Depths,* Sinclair's *The Jungle,* and Steinbeck's *The Grapes of Wrath.* The tune pointing out none would've been written if there wasn't some truth behind what was going on, that sometimes fiction is the only weapon in the arsenal to point out the cold, hard facts. How a few like to live at the expense of many, getting the many to always be thinking of God, while the few are always thinking about cash, that the reward for the few is always in the present, and the reward for the many is always in the future.

Darwin is in Town is another. The first line, "Go and inherit the wind, it's worth pile feces, and don't be paying any mind to the origin of species..." Pointing out that if Darwin was guilty of anything, it was putting down that progress is the natural direction of the species. That God is conceptual in the spirit and not literal in the body. That change comes in two packages: physical and spiritual.

And if God and Darwin have one thing in common, they are both really hard to understand. That it's more a question of where you are headed as opposed to where you came from. That if anything, God gives us progress, and Darwin, well, he just explains the cost.

That night, we were all captives, but not by the cats downstairs, but by the transistor on the table and the Radio Ventriloquist.

Towards the end of the broadcast, eventually, all made it to a bunk, except for Pipe, who stayed by the window. Each caught the comfort of laying back and closing their eyes and opening their ears, tasting the sweet irony of violation within incarceration - listening to the underground radio whilesmoking in bed.

And over the years, I've mentioned the message of those tunes in passing at cocktail parties and such. People have beenimpressed by my knowledge of the realist fiction writers Darwin, Dickens, and Marx.

I've always tried to explain the three sides of every coin and so on, to the point where some find me fairly articulate and educated. I never mentioned it all came from a night in jail as opposed to my university training. If anything, that nightserved me well over the years.

When I got up the day I got out, Pipe was still at the window.

He gave me a nod. "Down the road, Dart," and to a select few, this is what I go by: "Dart."

I never made mention to him of the ride that put meupstairs, and how Pipe knew to this day is still a mystery to me, and it's one of many. One thing is for sure: I was right all along.I had plenty to drop on a few cats once I caught up with them.

Looking back, the impact of the radio that night was on thesame level as Orson Welles' "War of the Worlds" back in the 30s. Pipe's *Radio Ventriloquist:* same intensity, smaller audience. The beauty being that I keep thinking just the cats in jail caught the show that night, but some cats at the filling stations or doing the third shift somewhere had to tune in; we weren't alone.

And like the rest, I have my moments of doubt. Sometimes, I wonder if the radio had any batteries and that maybe Pipe was a ventriloquist, and that's why he was standing by the window. The thoughts come and go. Had my allotted time with the Pipe, was ordained by him, and I caught up with every cat that I wanted to drop this on.

It wasn't too long after I got out the *Radio Ventriloquist* album showed up in the mail, Special Delivery with no returnaddress.

I remember ripping the brown wrapping paper off. When I got finished, I saw the gray floor model radio pictured on the black background. The design below the knobs covering the speakers represented the barred window; there was a dummy sitting on top of the radio. On the floor by the radio was a program that had written across it in white letters, "Radio Ventriloquist."

It was such a treasure. I turned on everyone I knew to the album. For weeks, more and more cats kept dropping by, day and night, to hear it. There was quite a pilgrimage for a while.Everyone wanted to borrow it, and after a while, it got to the point I put it in a safety deposit box. But as time went by, I lostthe key then stopped making payments. Eventually, the bank went under, and with it, the album. I tried to get it back, but it just faded from sight.

I'll just mention this in passing. When I went to throw the brown wrapping paper away is when I noticed the handwrittennote. It was on the inside, and I caught it by accident. It read, "Won't forget the time we were together." Always have had the feeling there was something feminine behind it and that hemeant to send it to someone else, that I got the album by accident. I still have the note.

About all I can say is Stovepipe blew in, and he blew out. I caught the prophet—the false and the true. If it's like every catputs down, that he cashed in overweight on a bus trying to getback to The Rib because his Comet faded, about the only thingI can add is it happened after *Radio Ventriloquist* was first heard on the underground radio in the county seat of Fairfield,Ohio. Those who tell you different don't know.

Album 5: Sticks to Bricks (According to Boat)

If I go on about it, don't expect a lot of details. It's not in my nature. See, in what I'm going to tell you, a lot of known details could still lead to a lot of trouble. I'll speak in general terms as to who, what, where. and when. I'll give you enough read between the lines.

I can tell you this. On a large body of water is where I caught Stovepipe. We were both moving north from city to country for different reasons, and both crossed the border into the "Land of the Maple Leaf" at the same time. On a ferry first to an island in Lake Erie and then on to the mainland.

After the trip is when I became known as "Boat" to the other cats. And where a lot cats think Spoon was the first to catch the Pipe, I got something to put on them. Spoon caught Pipe right after the army. I caught him right before.

The whole encounter started on one dock and ended at another, with nothing but water between the two. The whole time, never more than ten feet from this cat dressed mostly in crazy shades of black, white, and gray, wearing a patch over one eye.

Drawn to him like a nail to a magnet, to the point where I got to wondering about myself. And at that point in my life, the last thing I needed was to be distracted.

I had some things going on that one wrong move would set off a chain reaction that would mushroom me right into the solid bar motel for a long time. Had to be on top of my game because, with each move, I got deeper into something I'd wished I'd never gotten started.

But by the time I made the dock and loaded the trucks, it was too late to go anywhere but forward. I drove the last one on, parking it right next to a 63Comet. My wig was glued on when I was in the truck; that all changed when I got out, walking past the red and white Comet, thinking – who drives these anymore? Entering the twilight zone where you find out.

Four trucks in all, and just as planned, the others and I broke up and spread out. In fact, I never saw any of them; it was kind of strange because the crowd wasn't that big, and eventually, Icovered what seemed like every square inch of that boat with Pipe.

It was a relief after a while to figure out the magnetism. Justlike with everyone else, Stovepipe just appeared out of nowhere. A cat you never noticed at first, to a cat you couldn't break away from once you did notice, even if you wanted to.

Believe me, I'm not one to look at a man's ass, but the way he was leaning over the rail looking at the water, I couldn't help but notice the silver key dangling from his left cheek pocket. The way the sun caught it from where I was sitting onthe bench behind him, you could make out the word "Comet."It glowed in the sun. Had the car, and I now had the driver. Soearly in the game, that mystery was solved.

I wanted to start a rap, clearing my throat getting ready to speak, when I heard a loud click, and I froze up. The click came right after Pipe had reached inside his coat pocket with his lefthand.

He then turned from the rail and gave me a nod, hand still inside the coat like he was ready to pull something from it. And with all that I had going on, I had a pretty good idea what it might be – and that the game I'd been playing for the last six months was about to end. The clock had just run out, and I'd lost.

Remember it well that what was unfolding shouldn't come as any surprise—this cat was on my trail and tracked me down. The click was the hammer pulled back, and the driver was all about taking me in or blowing me away; didn't matter, and that he seemed to have all the details.

If panic and relief can happen at the same time, it was right at that moment. The moment I thought I was caught; glad the end had come – even though it wasn't what I'd hoped for. The jig was up, and I didn't seem to care. It was an amazing feeling and one I've never had again – one I never forgot. Somehow, I didn't mind being taken in by this cat.

And when I try to tell inside cats about this situation, all they want to know is what side the patch was on and if there was a musical note on it, and I tell them I was still too wrapped up in the click and the hand I couldn't see to even care, but there wasn't any note on it.

All I remember was staring at a one-eyed Jack getting ready to take me down. But that wasn't the case at all. Next thing that happened, Pipe returned to the rail, and I returned to the key dangling from his pocket. The key now made me think of jail and that it was all just a matter of time, and who is this cat?

All that could be heard were wind and waves. The time I was supposed to be studying maps and paper work – the plan – was being sucked up by an unanticipated situation.

I was locked up by what was in front of me as the ferry pushed on, and Pipe was locked on the water as if I weren't there. And I'm here to tell you that there might not be a Stovepipe if I would've gone with what was blowing through my mind after the click, and he turned his back. For a while, I was thinking of bending him over the rail and into the drink.

It took me awhile to figure out the jig wasn't up at all, and I tell the cats the first hour or so being around Stovepipe was no picnic.

When he turned from the rail to face me again, it all changed. I couldn't move. What he pulled out and held on me was a transistor radio or cassette tape recorder, something not much bigger than a king-size pack of smokes. Looking back, it was probably a little too early for the tape recorder, but who knows? One of the two, take your pick.

More than likely, it was a radio. I don't know; never thought much about what it was, never quit thinking about what came out of it. I know it's a problem for the chronologists, but that's the way it is.

I bring it up to point out to any cat that it doesn't matter whether *Stix To Bricks* was first heard on tape or the radio. I know I'm responsible for the debate going on in the inner circle. But then again, I might be the first to experience the doubt others have talked about.

Like maybe he did play all the instruments on his first album, or maybe he did transfigure one winter night. Maybe Miss America 1950 was his mom, and maybe there really weren't any batteries in the "shirt pocket" in Lancaster, Ohio. I've heard them all. I'm in the school, and what matters is what I heard and how it all came down. If it's that important, let's just say it was a radio and move on.

Stovepipe spoke for the first time. One word – "Tunes" – and that was it, he smiled and then sat down beside me. He set the volume to where you had to stretch your ears to catch what was coming from the 'king-size pack," and he placed it between us. And it took me a while to catch what was comingfrom it.

In short, what was coming from the pack was a voice. A voice that was hard to hear, describing the cat to my immediateleft, patch, color scheme, and his tunes (which I say to this day are pre-Beaufort). What was heard sounding like an all-pointsbulletin. One would have to be blind not to pick up who they were sitting next to.

My introduction to the Stovepipe was over the air waves, or magnetic tape, whatever, and what an introduction it was. After his one spoken word, he said a lot without saying a thing.

The water was calm, and the light reflected off it; there was a clear view for miles filled with soft colors. The king-size pack rapped on and became a "voice" you could now hear but barelyunderstand. And the "voice" called herself an "RV" – 'Radio Voice' – not a DJ, and not a ventriloquist – no matter how nicethe fit.

Gradually, the voice gave way to the "tunes," and the tunes covered my condition right down to every detail. I know what Spoon is talking about.

If you look at tunes from pop to rock, rhythm and blues, and country, what I caught was the last one mentioned: tunes about women trying to hold onto men, and the men trying to hold on to them, always something in between, another person, money, alcohol; everybody working hard and getting nowhere,hanging out at the wrong places and making bad decisions, trying to take care of the family.

The tunes were instrumentally tight and lyrically clear. Every cut had a moral of what was up the road if you didn't change.

And I remember at the time, I was all for change, had every intention of changing once I got out of what I was in. But whatI was in, I had to ride right to the end. I was in way too deep for any sudden change, like just walking away from it right then and there. Having the heat on me would be far better thansome of the cats I was dealing with tracking me down, and forsure, I didn't need both of them after me at the same time.

It was my first; I was in the third trimester of breaking the law hard. See, the birth of any crime goes through three phases: the plan, the crime, and the payoff (PCP), the hallucinogen thatallows you to picture pulling the crime off.

So far, I'd held up my end of the plan and the crime, but the payoff was making me nervous; a lot of bad things can happenin the last trimester. Being with the Pipe wasn't helping,looking back on when I caught *Stix To Bricks.*

The consummation of the crime happened one afternoon. A woman that I'd known ambushed me by a lake under a clear sky near some tall grass. I'd known her for years and all she'd been through. Walking up a hill, I looked at her, and in all theyears I'd known her, she never looked better.

And at that very moment, all I wanted was to be the best thing that ever happened to her. I won't tell you what I gave her there; it's not what you think. To this day, only two people know. She became the center of my universe - thin, tan, browneyes and dark hair, smart.

She was my motivation, won't say any more about her. Shenever knew she was behind it all. These were the thoughts running through my mind at the time, sitting next to the silent Stovepipe, listening to the 'pack' between us.

We weren't too far out when the tunes started to come in clearer. I first heard *Hardware*, a tune about a robbery, with a chorus… "six hundred miles down the road." I was struck by the irony; we had a place picked out six hundred miles down the road from the hill we walked up. The payoff was so important because of her and the place. And even though I gazed on smooth waters, the tune let me know I was entering dangerous waters.

Oh, it was a tune! It had more details than I cared to hear; a tune about moving contraband over the border. It was a tune with a last line that asked a question instead of giving an answer. "How'd it all turn out?" I gazed on out on the water, wondering if I was going to drown.

Throughout the plan and the crime, I had this mysterious melody running through my head, the only thing I didn't have were the words. Hearing the words with the melody of what I'd been doing for the past six months put me in a major tailspin.

I never related to a tune like that again. *Who, what, when,* and *where* were all there, along with all the details. Details like a huge hardware store, inside cats, a line on four trucks, and an over-the-border buyer running the biggest yard sale on the continent.

Details like the forged paperwork with five 'yards' right behind it, a uniform at the border in our pocket. The lyrics were all there, telling me the feelings I was starting to experience were just part of the payoff. Seemed the lyrics were giving it away for everyone to know.

The tunes played in sets of three, maybe four, then the voice. To a lot of cats, this puts *Stix To Bricks* first heard on radio and before the army. But the "king size pack," as it became known, was bigger than the "shirt pocket." I mean, over the years, they've knocked a lot of weight off the tape recorder. I could've been one of the first to catch the major reduction in size. I could have been listening to a tape of somepast broadcast. Who knows? Who cares? All I remember was the RV telling her audience to "Pipe On," and that's what I did.

Airwaves or tape, all I know is the RV rapped in different frequencies; you could only pick up part of what she was putting down. Probably the part she'd want you to catch, and then back to another set that came in crystal clear. That, in turn, would take me back to scenes of each phase of the crime.

A plan, in reality, made in a bar after more than one beer and consummated on a hill that, when it came off, came off like clockwork. Most would say this is good, but to the four of us involved, the feeling was more of a surprise and made it easy to move forward. Even though we knew the farther we went, the thinner the ice, but we could make it.

I remember in one set I caught *That Simple,* and it drove meto the wall - the wall where you can't deny what's going down,no matter how much you want to. That the unusual was gettingthe upper hand in what was happening around you, and it wason auto pilot.

See, the four of us didn't have a problem with the crime. We decided to take the inventory instead of the cash drawer; there was more gold on the floor than in the drawer. We didn'tmind a bit relieving the owner of the floor – that simple.

If anything, he had it coming for some of the deals he pulled. Had it coming acting the way he did because he was theonly game in town. How he treated and paid people. He acted like some Fortune 500 executive. Everything he did was about keeping himself rich and everyone around him poor. He wasn't about community; he was about cash. He brought it on by his own hand – that simple.

Then, somewhere down the line, I caught *Ruthless Business*. What else could it be about, other than a deal never meant to be fulfilled. In short, it was about acting like the boss, pulling the rug out from under someone.

Found a guy up north that had cash for what we could get, enough to make us think the cut for each was a lot, about five times our annual wages. So we bought five years for ourselveswith the floor.

We set up a dummy company and froze the floor, ordered everything he had at top dollar. Shipped it all to a rented warehouse. The day before it was supposed to all come down - all these orders were to be paid — we disappeared with his stuff, leaving a really confusing paper trail to cover our tracks. We robbed the place and vanished. And the best part, heard later on, he was under-insured.

And it wasn't like there wasn't any research and effort in what we did. Each of us created a new identity, found a new place to go, and started all over again. We all put some time behind it; all helped each other in covering the direction they wanted to take. We had some paperwork behind us to hide thetrails we took.

We knew we were the virgins and the owner, the whore, when it came to who could cheat who. We boned up and learned a lot from him before we went into motion. Yeah, *Ruthless Business* was about good cats going bad. And with each move, we were always surprised how easy it was getting.

In fact, it was like a well-hit ball heading for some far-off window - going a lot farther than you ever thought, maybe far enough to smash it, and you'd have to pay for it. You on the ground with no control over the flight you just initiated, awaiting the outcome. That's what the tunes were bringing out.

I had a lot riding on the flight of that ball. And the water that held my gaze put back right and wrong into the equation. Making the answer harder to get because what I was doing was right and wrong at the same time.

It felt right to take a shot; we were tired of getting shorted from the boss's end. We were tired of living in houses made of sticks while the boss lived in one made of bricks. But we were wrong with how we were going about it, no matter how deserving the target. And once we got the ball rolling, right or wrong didn't seem to matter anymore. Once we put the plan in motion, there was no way to stop what we were doing.

That's when I caught *Never Again,* and it leveled my head. I don't know about the others, but I didn't want to become what I was becoming, *That Simple, Ruthless Business, Never Again,* still play through my mind like the day I first heard them.

Stovepipe gave another nod, got up, and started wandering all over that boat. He put me in the awkward position of having to follow. And it struck me: here I thought the Pipe was on my trail, but it wasn't that way at all; I was on his.

I'd almost rather have jumped over the rail than have to follow him – almost. But Pipe wasn't hard to catch up to and didn't seem to mind my shadow next to his.

The pace was easy as the Pipe moved from stern to bow and back again with me on him like a cheap coat – tunes - the RV - and no breaking away, Stovepipe mentioned more than once from the 'king size pack' in his hand.

Some like to say *Sticks To Bricks* showed up before *Save Your Strength*. It's possible. I've caught the trivia question… "Of the six albums, which two are pre-Beaufort?" You'd be surprised at some of the answers, the fact is not even the inner circle knows the true chronology. The tunes are heard always on tape or radio; no one has ever watched an album spin and heard the tunes at the same time.

Now, I'd have to say where I differ from the others is that I heard Pipe's tunes before I heard his rap, and it was before he went into the army. And I know all about the Mounties.

******

The last set I caught from *Sticks to Bricks* eased my mind. In fact I can't tell you much about the last set other than the tunes became great background music to a plan so far running right on schedule. With the hardest part coming up, I was picking up some positive steam from this background music to get it over with and never pull something like this again.

The coast began to appear on the horizon, barely visible and still a long way off. And I formed a credo that I silently said to myself over and over again – "Get through, get paid, and get back." Back to that place six hundred miles down the road with the center of my universe and everything over and okay.

As I listened to this background music, each blink of my eyes became like the click from some View Master inside my head that showed what I could expect as I went forward. It wasa big help. So, as we moved around that boat, my confidence began to build. My footsteps telling me everything was going to work out, my credo becoming a silent mantra with each step – determined to make it happen.

This background music from the last set guided us to the rail again. There was nothing but water and the far-off horizonas we gazed at what was in front of us. Each in our own way wondering what the far off horizon held for us, what form of fate waited.

It was ironic in a way, our minds clouding over in thought and the view from the rail so clear. If anything, the weather wasperfect and, after a while, helped put the thoughts in order.

I put my forearms on the rail and leaned over, looking straight down about twenty feet to the surface of the water. The move spooked Stovepipe; the lean looked a little risky to him. Then he looked at me, the water, and then the far-off coast, asking, "You hip to the dip? You make it with the water?"

It took a moment for me to translate, and I nodded back. "Yes, I swim – I swim good." - just catching at the end the hayseed sound of my answer, like I was ready to go over the rail to prove the point. I know the language Noose talks about.

Finally, a rap began to unfold, and the Pipe eased into a smoke, continuing a line of questioning about swimming, ending by asking, "You ever pull a cat from the drink?" Now,I could've told Pipe I had, but I hadn't, so my answer was moreabout how I could, as opposed to if I ever had.

Right from the start, it wasn't hard to figure out Pipe had a thing about water. Pipe threw out, "Water does so many hip things, but it can take you out at a drop of a hat. Doesn't care if it grows crops or overruns its banks to kill the cats it just fed – doesn't care about good or bad, it's just water."

Told Pipe the same thing could be said about fire. Pipe nodded, exhaling a fine cone of smoke that was punctuated with, "I know about fire. Dig it's about *up* and *out*, fire doesn't burn water *up*, water puts fire *out*, control the water and you control fire. Same thing with good and evil – as good goes *up*, evil goes *out*, not *down*. See *down* means it could go *up*, again, *out* means gone. So you want a spiritual water level to control the fire that is in each of us." Somehow, what he was saying all made sense.

The Pipe placed the "king-size pack" on the rail between us again, with the voice of the RV barely audible and breaking up at times, the sound of the water complementing what was coming from the pack in a strange and pleasant way, pleasant static, if that's possible.

I was still wrestling with how all the tunes I'd heard fit my situation. I was in the mood to start asking some questions. I wanted to know how he came up with some of these tunes. Maybe he had tailed me the last six months; to this day, I still sometimes wonder.

And what's really strange, I felt I'd heard the melodies of those tunes blow through my wig the past six months starting with the plan, heard all of them, just the melodies, not the words. Felt that way from the first tune I heard, wanted an explanation for all my strange feelings. As it turned out, I never got to ask a single question.

I've run into a few people who have a thing about water; none came close to Stovepipe. If I know one thing about the Pipe for sure, it's a fact he couldn't swim. A body of waterbigger than a bathtub took him right to the edge.

And anybody that could swim seemed to amaze the Pipe. Like they had some sort of power. Anybody that could crawl on top of a large body of water had some type of spiritual gift, moving them closer to the Naz, who walked on water.

That they somehow understood what all religions know: that the true purpose of water is to give life, to be consumed, and to cleanse. One is internal, the other external; water takes care of the inside and outside of us, which is why it always needs to be at hand and respected for what it can do.

My suggestion to any cat that runs into the Stovepipe is thatshe or he brings up the fact that they can swim that they can deal with water. What you risk is being treated like a prophet and played like an instrument on one of his finer cuts on one ofhis better albums. That's what happened to me.

After a while, at the rail, everything I'd done in the last six months unfolded to the point that if Pipe didn't have every detail, he had it now. It was an effortless core dump. And at thesame time, I couldn't help but feel the cat that caught my confession had something on the same scale going on, which, in the end, I knew absolutely nothing about.

I gave him everything on me but had nothing on him. Andhere's the thing: while we were at the rail, Stovepipe did ninetypercent of the rapping. All he talked about was the water. He took water to the point where it had to be feared, had to be respected like it is God. Putting it down with more conviction as the shore drew near.

When we hit the coast, everything changed. I had my deal, and he had his; only difference, he knew everything about mine. Talk to the Pipe if you want to know who we knocked off, who was involved, and who was at the other end. And it took some time, after the fact, to figure out what Stovepipe had going on. It took a while before I figured it out.

When we hit the coast, the last thing Pipe ever asked me was if I had two "C" notes for a "J. C. Calhoun." My only answer was, "What?" He shot back, "Can you break a two hundred?" This was when I first learned such a bill existed.

A two hundred dollar bill faced with President John C. Calhoun, and I took two of the five one hundred dollar bills under the paperwork from my truck and replaced them with one John C. Calhoun. Never had seen a two hundred dollar bill, but it looked pretty authentic, looked more legitimate than the two one hundred dollar bills I gave him. I never questioned him on it.

Last conversation ended in that transaction, and we got into our rides. Last time I ever saw him. He left me with my mind wrapped around all that had happened on deck.

My emotions were independent of my thoughts, like Motor's, as I started up my truck, never once checking to see if the others had made it. But right after I fired up, I heard them fire up, and everything was working out as I put all the paperwork in order and the bills under it right next to me on the seat. Never saw one of them on the boat, and yet here they were firing up with me just as planned.

Lit a smoke and clicked the View-Master in my wig, and saw the border way before I was off the boat, Pipe in front of me in his Comet. Everything was moving fast and on target.

Stovepipe pulled the Comet off the ferry, and my truck and three more were right behind him. It was soon after that what was expected went from a fastball to a changeup.

We found a line at the border, which provided the last few minutes of solitude before the big deception. Everything I had in order for this defining moment. I took a Calvinist view that if we didn't get caught, at this moment, that the whole deal was okay with God, that it was preordained.

What happened next was a drive-in movie. The tail lights of the Comet glowing like the lights off some spaceship. The silhouette of Stovepipe at the controls filled my front windshield. The spaceship had just landed, rolling the window down to make first contact.

The agent stood outside studying what was before him, and Pipe took the time to light a smoke, cracking the eight-slash Zippo as he held it in one hand between thumb and forefinger, and with a short snap, a quick burst of fire lit his smoke. The agent jumped back for a second; it happened so fast that, for a moment, it had all the characteristics of a shooting. This was the first impression my vision gave me. Saw the burst and the agent jump, then closed my eyes.

When I opened them, the agent gave the signal, and within seconds, five to six Mounties came out of nowhere, moving like hornets, covering the headlights, taillights, and doors, ready to sting.

They were agitated. They had something on Pipe. The feeling they were ready to ask all the questions about what Pipe had going down was inescapable. Their look was beyond stern, and they weren't playing around. It was a situation where the right answer would be the wrong answer. And these cats were all about getting the right answers one way or the other. Through it all, Stovepipe smoked as if he were calmly waiting for a haircut in some downtown barber shop.

I'd be lying if I told you I wasn't heading for a major panic attack with all the uniforms in front of me. The Royal Canadian Mounties filled my windshield and me, sitting on four trucks of hot merchandise.

It was a real blast of paranoia. "What if they start asking questions? What if they're really crowding Pipe about me?" I started to ask myself. Every thought I had was unpleasant.

An agent came to my window and banged on it to get my attention and broke the spell. It was our uniform. When he got my attention and the window down, the only thing out of his mouth was, "Paperwork!" Nothing more, he wanted us out of there—fast—and I was more than willing to work with him on this.

He stepped back, counted the trucks, walked back, and put the paperwork inside the cab, letting the bills fall into my lap. He gave me the look that today was not the day for him to be holding anything extra. He then directed us to another gate, and within a few minutes, we were out of there and on our way. To make a long story short, from that point, I got over, got paid, and got back.

Tried later on to pay him, but he'd dropped off the radar. I made an honest effort, but I sure wasn't going to make it my life's work.

In the end, we were five hundred above a sweet deal, an extra $125 each – which actually turned into an extra $75 when you consider the "Calhouns."

******

Stovepipe, on the other hand, stayed at the border with the Mounties. And I know there are a lot of cats putting down all kinds of raps about the matter.

The only fact I can put down is that the part about the Mounties is real, saw enough uniforms that day to know they weren't playing around; they were going to keep him for a while. They captured him.

For what, who knows? Probably most comfortable with Dart's idea that Pipe got nailed for some of his cuts on *Radio Ventriloquist*. That someone 'downstairs' didn't like what they heard, forgetting that protest doesn't come without some truth.

That a deal was made between the two governments to pick Stovepipe up, rough him up a little, send him back, and then over to get him killed and out of the picture.

Dart is almost at the point where what he heard in jail in Fairfield County, Ohio, was a recording too, not a radio show, almost, but not quite. He won't come all the way round because this causes problems with the chronology.

If they think Fairfield was the first, to me, that can't be because *Radio Ventriloquist* was in Beaufort. And there's a wing out there that believes Pipe had all these albums done before anyone heard them and let them out whenever he felt like it – maybe, but who cares? Back to Dart's idea about the Mounties, it makes as much sense as anyone's.

But let me put my angle on all of this. Stovepipe didn't have any problems with the draft; he wasn't heading north because of that. He knew the wind was out there could blow on him just like any other cat, and it did.

He accepted it, in the end, he got through, got paid, and gotback and never had a problem with those who didn't accept it.It's not as romantic as everyone makes it out to be. He wasn't trying to avoid anything or to make a statement; no he was detained over money issues. That's my angle.

See, it wasn't until sometime later I found out there aren't any John C, Calhoun's; there aren't any two hundred dollar bills. Pipe was enough to overcome the intuition I first had, soit really wasn't much of a surprise. More a feeling of I should've known better.

That John C. Calhoun was vice president twice but never president. Pipe never counterfeited any money; he invented it – the two hundred dollar bill – and didn't have any trouble passing them.

Maybe the Mounties were more interested in this; I know it's less romantic, but to me more probable. The 'downstairs boys' might go after someone for the tunes they put out, but for sure, they'll go after someone for the bogus bills they put out.

I had a friend who had the *Sticks to Bricks* album. How he came across it was as big a mystery as Stovepipe. What is beyond strange is he was on the boat with me. All he can tell me is some cat handed it to him as he got in the truck. Some cat wearing an eye patch.

I saw it one day at his house, not more than a week after wesplit up. It had a white background, sticks laid out in black, spelling 'sticks,' the 'T' in 'to' was also in stick format, the 'o' in 'to,' began the gray bricks, laid out to spell 'bricks.' The black sticks and gray bricks even against the white background.

The day I found it, he was in a big hurry to go somewhere and wouldn't let me borrow it. I've always felt the album wasmeant for me, but never told him. A week after the find, he gotkilled on his bike. I asked his wife about the album, and she told me it's in his coffin. There are times when I seriously think about getting it.

And like everyone else, I've caught all that's out there about Stovepipe's weight, the chick, the bus, and that he's gone. And I believe he's on the other side, but then he always was. I'm not really sure he made the side most of us are on.

And where a lot of cats think they got the Stovepipe down, it's really the other way around. And on the scale of solid, we're the sticks, and he's the bricks – that's all I have to say.

Album 6: Good Wood (According to Book)

One of the largest ports on the Great Lakes has a museum that opened for the first time in 1916. Placed in proper proportion to the landscape, there is a building of fine marble with large windows and bronze doors. It has several floors and many rooms. On these floors and within these rooms are the paintings, sculptures, writings, weapons and relics of the past. It is a monument to the good and bad efforts made by those who came before us. A cultural bank that shows what we've saved.

On one of these floors, and in a few rooms, early 1973, I saw and heard Stovepipe. Not only the Stovepipe but the *Big Notes.* Live.

One Saturday afternoon in that museum, I caught the anthology of everything he'd put out. The cuts he liked from every album, plus two new cuts, and he called it *Good Wood.* The Whitman Sampler of his work, from *Save Your Strength* to *Sticks to Bricks*, pre-Beaufort to Beaufort, for the chronologists.

I saw all the displays and mentioned in them all the characters who played a role, right down to the Rib behind *Bagpipes and Bongos.* The two new cuts, the 'good wood' added to the fire of the old cuts, the fire, heating a branding iron that had your mind as its final destination. The Pipe hit me like an A-Bomb that day, and it mushroomed from there.

Like to get it out of the way—upfront—so it won't interfere with what I have to say. Pipe showed up wearing the patch with the note - don't remember which eye, but probably over both at one time or another, he was smooth and there all day probably moved it more than once.

He wore his signature tri colors, black and white wing tips, white pants, gray shirt, black suspenders, wide black- and white-striped silk tie.

The shoes were a work of art; the pants and shirt were tailored, the stripes on the tie angled. All the pleats were in the right places. And it's strange because most know him by his colors; few will tell you what he looks like. No two descriptions of him ever match; only his colors match in every description. To me, he wasn't young or old, thin or fat, just there in three-D.

He played only one note from the Tube to start each cut and then let the *Big Notes* wrap themselves around that kickoff and run it back, which they did every time. Everything I caught changed my direction as I was overtaken by an obsession to learn everything there was about this cat. He was that clean.

Like to get this out of the way too – I'm the book Spoon started, and that's what they call me, "Book." I'm not like Spoon, Noose, Motor, Dart, or Boat. I've heard about them, they've heard about me. We've heard about each other from the cats to the base of ten. We've talked to each other and corresponded, but we've never met face to face. Unlike the others, Pipe never named me. I never said a single word to Stovepipe. He never spoke to me the day I saw him, and what separates me from the rest is I'm the only one to ever see and hear him play. I became 'Book' by being referenced by others in my conversations and correspondence with them about my day with Stovepipe in the museum and what I became from that day forward.

They've all met. And it's not like we haven't tried to get together, but at the last minute, every set-up with the five would fall apart. How they fell apart is another story. Let's just say there's a force out there that just won't allow this to happen.

From that day in the museum to now and on into the future my obsession has been and is to own every object the man is willing to sell. I was way ahead of the game when it came to bundling Stovepipe's possessions. Now all of a sudden what I've been doing is important to a lot of people.

This has been primary to me and financed by my secondary obsession to make money – straight or crooked. How successful have I been? Well, I have all six tapes of the Pipe's albums. And they didn't come easy; they came hard; I've seen a lot of blind alleys, but I've caught some that got me to where I want to be.

******

How this all came about was on a Saturday when I had absolutely nothing to do and no one to do it with. Got up feeling okay, considering the night before, and whoever was with me was gone. I'm sure I know her, though. I know one thing: if they let you talk to them long enough, you can talk them into anything.

Went to the diner a half block from my place, bought a big breakfast, finished it up with a few cups of coffee and some smokes, reading the paper. After that, the ball got rolling.

Actually, the whole episode came together by mistake. The avalanche to come had a gradual beginning. I had drifted to the section of the paper that put down the cultural happenings in Browns town that day. A section I hardly ever read. What held my interest for some strange reason was a coming exhibit entitled *From Canals to Railroads*, early to mid-1800, at the museum.

I didn't catch the fact the coming attraction started the following Saturday. The word 'coming' blew by me like a fastball. *From Library to Radio – And What Happened In Between*, all part of the museum's "From" series of exhibits was at the museum. It just didn't register, even though it was mentioned more than once that this was the last Saturday. My mind got stuck on the coming exhibit as being the current exhibit.

I can tell you as I made my plans to catch *From Canals to Railroads*, it turned out to be like the waiter coming back and telling you they're out of what you ordered and what you got as a replacement, making you forget what you ordered in the first place. *From Library to Radio – And What Happened In Between;* a meal I've only started to digest.

And since I hadn't been in a museum since I was a kid, I decided I was going. "Put me down," I said to myself. Having no idea what I was about to catch, thinking one thing, finding out another.

Took it to the point I started asking for directions. The first two guys I talked to, well, one said it was north, the other south, and if they gave me any information at all, it was they had no idea.

The second guy I talked to kept referring to the museum as the "closet," and what a waste of money. He really didn't want to give it any support by giving directions, asking over and over again, "Why would you want to go there?" Like there was something wrong with me. What a waste of time.

It wasn't until I asked a woman that I got something I could use. She knew exactly how to get there. And if she was anything, she was engaging.

We began a conversation as we waited in a short line to pay our bill. She opened her purse to write down everything I needed to know. But before I got that information, I had to go through how amazed she was that I'd been in town for as long as I said and not been to the museum, ending by asking, "This is the first time you're going to the museum?"

Implied I was some sort of cultural desert she had just discovered. She then went on to give me the directions to the library at no extra charge. "Suppose you haven't been there either?" Like she was writing me a ticket.

It's not like I was as desolate as she thought; she only gave directions to two locations. I could give her directions to at least fifteen. The only difference, her locations were a museum and library; mine would be bars and restaurants. For some reason, I found her annoyingly pleasant.

She also pointed out that she had been to the current exhibition and that I'd be a changed person once I caught it. She began to explain how overcome she was by it. This was right at the time I was starting to notice how attractive she was becoming, the back of my mind moving forward, saying, "Forget the museum – make it with the chick." …Stopped paying attention to her and began to concentrate on this.

I didn't catch most of what she was saying. She was like the paper; me not paying attention to what was out there in black and white. All I was looking for was an opening. It was a strange day of overlooking the obvious.

Began to think I could talk exhibits. Next pause she took, I was going to irrigate the desert in front of her by giving her all I knew about canals and railroads. She was about to find out it was more than the average cat. I did Ohio State start to finish, and canals and railroads had come up – infrastructure.

She'd taken me to the point that I was willing to bring out my 'A' game, thinking if she dug canals and railroads, so did I, even though they never came up once if I had been listening.

The opening came as she ran out of breath in her renewed excitement about the exhibit, and I jumped in. Began to core dump for about five minutes, nonstop, on the city of Cleveland and how the canals and railroads were the "infrastructure" that moved a lot of Northern iron into the Civil War.

Made her aware Cleveland is an ethnic city of Anglo, Germanic, Slavic, and Afro–American people whose ancestors worked the canals and railroads. Everyone was involved in its development.

I talked about the Erie Canal and the Baltimore & Ohio Railroad. It was all first-rate: proper grammar, best I could do, good eye contact, and a lot of smiles. No two ways I was attracted – she had great eyes.

And when I ended, she gazed at me expressionless for what seemed like forever. Drawing me to the conclusion I'd turned the corner, and we could move on to phone number, where she lived, and what she did.

But then she gave her head a quick shake and, without a word, walked away. It wasn't until later I found out why. Where'd the canals and railroads fit in with the exhibit she saw? There was no recovery. I couldn't follow her; her eyes had the glaze. And at the time, I was surprised and a little hurt.

But then again, she did leave me the way to the museum in her own hand, so I moved on. My hurt pride rationalizing, "I got what I wanted from her," trying to ignore the fact I sure would have liked to have gotten more.

******

At that time, everything was a deal for me. Everything had to have something I could wrap myself around when it was over. At that time, I was all about pawn shops and sheriff's sales and making good money off the misfortunes of others. It was easy, mostly legal, and I was good at it. Until the museum that was my direction, she was right; I was a changed person after I caught the exhibit.

After eating breakfast, reading the paper and the episode of getting the directions in the diner, I paid my bill and left. Stepped outside and got my bearings from some landmarks. Seems someone said the museum was about seventeen blocks north. I couldn't remember if it was a total of seventeen blocks, with a few right and left-hand turns, or a straight-line distance. It was north and seventeen blocks; I'd figure it out. All I had to do was decide if I would walk or drive.

My place was in the opposite direction, and the day was raw. I was leaning south to go get the car. But then I got to thinking a city block was about a football field, close to one hundred yards, seventeen blocks, seventeen hundred yards times three feet, 5,100 feet – less than a mile by 180 feet or sixty yards. The seventeen blocks sounded greater than the actual distance. It was first down for the walk after the measurement. It would be good for me.

Well, I'd walk under one condition: my gloves had to be in my coat. I'd taken one look out the window before I left for breakfast, and everyone had on their heavy coat. I lit a smoke, got mine out and put it on for the first time since the past winter, everyone letting me know I'd need it for the half-block trek to the diner.

It would now be on the peg, by the door, probably for the next three months. Now, there had been years when I left my gloves in my winter coat and years where I hadn't. Wouldn't expect anyone from the South to understand, but if you're from the North, you know what I'm talking about; it's always nice to put the winter coat on and find the gloves.

I drifted into a mindset where if the gloves were in the pockets, it was going to be a good year. All I had to do was ride out the last three months of this year, if they were there, and blow into the next year with everything going my way. I was making a big deal out of the gloves being there.

Probably in the past five winters found the gloves with the coat two times, so it wasn't an even bet: forty percent on the side of good karma and sixty percent on the side of bad karma.

I got lost in the thought and decided to play it out. I started by slowly getting the hands in the right position. The pockets became holsters holding the guns I was looking for in my mental gunfight with fate. Had to be a two-handed draw, too; one glove was the same as having no gloves. You'd have to do what you wanted to avoid. You'd have to buy a pair. So, in this little head game, it came down to how fate was going to treat me in the future. I felt I had a lot riding on the draw. I began to take on the appearance I was in Dodge City instead of Cleveland.

My hands began to pick up speed, and at the moment of truth, there they were! It was a great natural rush, like getting hit by the velvet freight train, like I was a little too quick for Mr. Probability in our mental gunfight.

And I did it just that way. The guy coming towards me on the sidewalk – well, he came to a sudden stop and took a step back when I went for my gloves. For a moment, I stopped him in his tracks. He gave me a serious look and then eventually moved on. I didn't pay it any mind to how I startled him. I wastoo wrapped up in the good fortune about to come my way.

******

I stopped and lit a smoke before I put the gloves on. Headednorth block by block, and sometime during a second smoke, the museum came into view.

As I walked towards it, the reflecting pools, walkways, steps and plants worked well with each other for a cold, gray, late autumn day. It was like walking within the black, gray andwhite shades of a well-composed pencil drawing. To the pointwhere one could imagine what it would look like in the light of different seasons; what colors would come out. The landscape was beginning to prime the imagination. What first appeared small on the horizon was becoming more immense with eachstep.

Hit that last smoke hard before entering the museum, hard enough to take me through an afternoon, an afternoon ofroaming halls and rooms. And I remember once inside, the desire to smoke left me. So I bought a little time there, part of the good fortune. See, normally, with the time I spent in the museum, I'd have smoked half a pack on a Saturday afternoon.So it was kind of like I banked a half-pack for the future.

And the way I started to behave, you'd have thought what I'd smoked weren't ordinary smokes – but they were. Got stuck at the door, both literally and mentally, how big and heavy it was, and how easy it moved, how it was made, and how it was set, its balance. Opened and closed it enough times to draw the attention of an employee.

I explained my fascination as best I could and got an understanding nod. Then I asked where the exhibit was on canals and railroads. "Next week," he replied. "What?" was all I could come up with, and before I could ask any more questions, he answered, "'From library to radio, and what happened in between' is concluding this week. Next week, from canals to railroads, will start and continue for the next eight weeks."

It was at this point the "eyes" from the coffee shop popped back into my wig, and the mystery of the glazed look was solved. As the employee continued on about the current exhibition, I got stuck on her for a moment, just like I got stuck on the door. And had to laugh at the mystery I'd just solved. The laughter met with a smile as he continued on about the current exhibit.

I pick him up again as he started rapping on about the cat that put the exhibition together, ending by telling me he'd seen the exhibit on more than one occasion. He even took a day of vacation the last time. And the cat he was talking about was always referred to as "Stovepipe," and that was the first time I'd ever heard of the Pipe.

******

Found out where the exhibit was and began to wander in its direction. I got sidetracked twice, once in front of George Bellow's

Stag at Sharkey's and then in a room filled with armor, shields, and swords.

In the first, I got wound up in the color and imagery of thetwo fighters and the crowd behind them. The colors made it a one-dimensional sculpture of two forces going after each otherthat left me spellbound.

In the second, I didn't stop, but I circled the room more thanonce. Every item displayed showed the weight of protection and destruction, thick breastplates and two-handed swords. And I felt a sense of my continuing good fortune that I didn't live in that space of time where life was probably violent, painful, and short for most.

There was a lot I wanted to see as I wandered towards the reason I'd come in the first place. I was getting sidetracked. I'dhave to come back.

Felt crowded and worried about the time I was spending, that enjoyment doesn't come without a price. I felt I was wasting time when actually I was enjoying it, but made it a point not to stop anymore and move to what I'd come to see – the exhibit. I remember few people filled the rooms that held the paintings and the weapons, and I always felt a little crowded with them around.

When I found myself on the upper floor, in the halls and rooms that held *From Library to Radio and What Happened In Between,* it all changed. On that floor, one couldn't turn in any direction without seeing people, yet at the same time, I felt like I had the whole place to myself.

And I began to wander with them through the exhibit. I didn't read one write-up by myself. It seemed like ten people were always around me. And it was like everyone read the information at the same rate, at the same level, and ended at thesame time.

Then nods and comments were made, everyone had something to say, and everyone was listening. Probably the closest I've ever come to a spellbinding experience. It seemed several groups of about ten people moved from room to room like small herds feeding on good pasture, experiencing the balance of nature - human nature.

It was set up this way, all by Stovepipe. There were ten stops. I spent a minimum of twenty minutes at each, except thelast one, that was the fastest hour of my life. The most fluid thing I'd ever traveled through, everything in perfect balance, like the door. In a little over four hours, the time it would takeme to pound down a half-pack of smokes, I changed. In that small interval of time I picked up a lot. Still carrying the weightit's made me strong.

******

I can put you in every room. I haven't forgotten any of them. Those ten stops covered 189 years of American history. And it started out with the concept of nation-building. And what would history be if we didn't have the dates? The dates some learn, and some don't. When you find yourself in a well-lit room trimmed in off-white referencing the year 1731, you'dbe at the first stop.

This would be the year given to the first circulating library in Philadelphia, testing the theory more information is better than less for any population how this library was the first distribution source of information to the public on many topics. That if you wanted to know something there was a place whereyou could go read about it. It had its roots in the Colonies. When it comes to nation-building, open libraries are at the foundation; Rome had thirty libraries. The library in Philadelphia operated forty-five years before the American Revolution, and in 1776, Philadelphia was a hotbed of revolutionary thinking. If anything, libraries created a demand for literacy in society, an important contribution. Thought at one time I'd had a library card; by the time I left the first stop, I thought I should get another one. I had the directions.

From one display to the next, what unfolded was a map where great distances between destinations were beginning to be covered in a shorter amount of time as you moved down the road. And that if you took the first ninety-nine years from the first circulating library and stopped at that destination, you might find yourself working or riding on the steam railroad, and if you were me, you'd find yourself in a dark green room trimmed in white oak with a gold finish telling you all about it, the second stop.

The date given 1830, the year the Baltimore & Ohio started steaming passengers and freight here and there, one of the outcomes of the ninety-nine-year period when America went to the library and read. The transportation network was open for business. The display went into great depth that this all happened in less than a century. One year short of a century wasn't enough to keep me from rounding up and calling it a century. With or without the one year, the time frame is impressive.

The exhibits were becoming like small towns in time, with the right amount of space between them to let your mind unwind from one stop to the next. Three years down the road from Baltimore & Ohio, in 1833, Oberlin College in Ohio established coeducation. And this would be the third stop.

A room filled with old photographs, books, notebooks, pens and paper on desks under the right amount of light. A room setting the stage for the benefits that followed from educating the two 'true' populations, the *total* population, on the same level. That as we moved on, its importance should not be overlooked, that 1833 was a very important year.

At this stop, I said to myself, "So okay, from the first circulating library to coeducation is one hundred and twoyears, and the big thing that happened between the two was therailroad." This time, I rounded down and came to the conclusion I'd always call it a century. So, a century from the first circulating library, we got both the railroad andcoeducation. That as the movement of freight and passengers opened up, the need for literacy expanded on the *two true populations* to operate the network. It was all falling together.

******

That century, or ninety-nine years or one hundred two years, covered in the first three exhibits was a preface of what was to follow because 1833 became the baseline year for the remaining exhibits, the year of coeducation.

This started in a fine, finished, trimmed-stone room with an arched entrance, 1847 carved into the keystone, the fourth exhibit and the first display referencing the new baseline year. It began, "Within fourteen years of the first coeducational school, the first postage stamp was issued." Then went on to how the country began to communicate, pen and paper correspondence; reading and writing essential. The glass case before us displayed a variety of envelopes, stamps, and lettersfrom 1847 on, each year showing the growth in distribution.

Twelve years down the road, at the fifth exhibit, in a room accented with heavy timbers and tools, you were introduced to the steam and oil relationship, the source of power behind everything. The relationship, where first steam delivered the power, and oil was just a lubricant. And the exhibit pointed to a thin irony that as the need for steam increased, so did the need for oil. Then, kerosene came along to light the lanterns. The first commercial oil well showed up in Titusville, Pennsylvania, 1859. And as the years pulled away from that date, the relationship changed; in fact, it ended; oil became power, lubricant and light.

Terms like "Oil Baron" came into use, terms from autocratic, feudal societies. Awareness grew, and concentrated wealth could create or return to a society that benefited the barons the most. There was a period of monopoly, the 'company store,' a period of exploitative capitalism, where the biggest part of the pie went to few. Profit defined by long hours and low wages. No income tax, no unions, these pioneer capitalists didn't want to work with labor; they were in a position to own labor. Concentrated wealth was beginning to be something to watch.

The theme of heavy wood and tools carried on into the sixth exhibit, only with nine-pound hammers and eight-inch spikes. And it talked about the offspring of steam and oil, and that was the Transcontinental Railroad. The birth took place in Promontory, Utah, 1869, Thirty-six years from coeducation; the country had the big hook-up. And it became apparent that it was no longer a North, South thing, but now an East, West thing, Atlantic at one end, Pacific at the other, Asia at one end, Europe at the other for our goods.

Ten years after the "big hook up" and forty-six years from the baseline, you found yourself at the seventh exhibit – Mr. Frank Woolworth's Five & Dime. It was full of interesting merchandise brought by the railroad, and was the morning of big business in the garden of distribution, pricing, cash flow, and insurance, the nickel, dime economy. And it started in 1879; he had stores in Utica, New York, and Lancaster, Pennsylvania, at first, then all over.

I concluded that within the first fifty years of coeducation, we had the dime store, and I came from a generation where everyone had been to the dime store. In fact, we watched it die.

The eighth exhibit put you in the fine wood offices, furnished with expensive furniture, of the Home Insurance Company of Chicago, Illinois. And if the company was known for anything, it was that it built and occupied the first skyscraper. Ten stories were built in 1885, and a few years later they added two more stories. So, fifty-two years from baseline, we had the skyscraper. And the direction of the development of big cities was up, not out. The skyscrapers were space savers, concrete Tupperware.

It was also at this stop that you began to pick up the music coming from another room. The music had always been in the background. Now, it was beginning to take the foreground. And as you moved to the ninth exhibit, which housed a display of leather helmets, gloves, and jackets accented nicely by a set of goggles and long white scarves, the music was beginning to take off.

On one wall was a large wooden propeller; below it, a picture of Eddie Rickenbacker, America's first Ace, and a bi-plane. The write-up that followed mentioned the time the first Transcontinental

Air Mail route was established between New York and San Francisco in 1920. At seventy-three, the postage stamp went airborne.

Not only did you get air mail in 1920, but you also got radio, and that was huge. On October twenty-seven, 1920, out of Pittsburgh, the first licensed station, KDKA. First station licensed to give the news. Antennas began to fill the landscapeto provide the best reception.

The music from the next room, a nice sampling of everything ever played over the airwaves from 1920 on. The music is flavored by the works of Gershwin, Copeland, Bernstein, Dorsey, and Goodman, just to name a few.

I'd passed through all the exhibits did all 189 years; from the circulating library established in 1731 to the radio, KDKAlicensed in 1920, Philadelphia to Pittsburgh. The trip changedme.

And I have to tell you, as this all sunk in from Oberlin College 1833 to KDKA 1920, and the tunes in the background coming in clearer, with little resistance I became an eighty- seven-year-old man. Born the year of coeducation that, after fourteen could tell you where the post office was. After age twenty-six could talk about oil wells. That sometime after the Civil War, around age thirty-six, I rode the transcontinental railroad. At forty-seven had already been to the Five & Dime and, by fifty-three, had a policy with the Home Insurance Company. Felt this right to the bone.

The feeling continued to where I could go back to when thefirst stamp came out, to when it went air mail. Overcome by the feeling I'd lived it, not only could you ride coast to coast –you now could fly it. Everything from really young to really old began to overwhelm my thoughts. One in particular, not a lot of souls, but some caught that interval of time, 1833 to 1920.

And as that thought matured, I found myself in front of a display of photography from this period. There were four pictures in all of two men and a write-up on each man.

But before I get into that, it's interesting to note that the pictures were on loan from the Stovepipe family collection - "Stovepipe" one word, not two, like it was a legitimate last name – "Mr. Stovepipe, Ed Stovepipe, the Stovepipe family upthe road." For the chronologist, Stovepipe just might not be a nickname but a last name, just something to keep in mind.

Back to the display, the write-up pointed out they were theonly known photos of the two. After reading it, you find out here were two men born the year of the postage stamp, whose first big stop was the Civil War, being eighteen and nineteen when it ended. One lived to be one 109, the other one 112. They fought against each other, the last Civil War Veterans – Albert Woolson and John Salling. They caught the big hookup, airmail, and a lot more. And I have to tell you, I have their photographs. Took a lot of research, donations, memberships and cash to get them, but I got them.

******

The next stop was the big payoff. I felt like some old bi- plane looking for a place to land. I found it when I spotted about ten chairs in front of a small stage that had a display of microphones and instruments against a background of vintage phonographs, records and radios. The tenth stop. I thought it was a display.

No one was on the stage. You had enough time to sit in yourchair and contemplate John Salling and Albert Woolson, mentally catching your breath. That if you were either, by the end you had to wonder – people flying around and voices coming out of wooden boxes.

The contemplation ended when I caught another photo on the stage, just enough in view to picture a band. It was compelling enough to get up for a closer look. The only information given, it was a band of midgets from Akron, Ohio, circa 1940. I'm also going to tell you I now have a copy of that photograph. I know who's in it.

But getting back to the stage, the next thing I remember was the light hitting the microphones, and there he was, working the shadows, surrounded by the *Big Notes*. The seats were taken, and everyone watched each other take them. When there was complete silence and everyone looked up, Stovepipe stepped into the light and began to speak, thanking everyone for attending the exhibit in his own smooth language, which, for the most part, I can only paraphrase.

"Dig the crazy path to this place, always good to check the dipstick of time; you chair cats, you now circulating cats of ten - thanks for making this gig." That's straight from the Pipe. And what followed was a lesson in civics that went right back to the first three exhibits: the preface, the circulating library (distribution of knowledge), the railroad (distribution of goods) and the demand for literacy and coeducation. Literacy is defined as being able to read, write, and calculate.

And you couldn't catch whether Pipe was putting down that all the progress in the first one hundred two years from 1731 to 1833 was due to, or in spite of, the French and Indian War along with the American Revolution thrown in for good measure. One war and one revolution, and you couldn't pick up whether the progress over the one hundred two years was due to, or in spite of, human conflict.

"Let me detail this ride for you." And it was like he made individual eye contact with everyone who was sitting in front of him and was talking just to them. He went on to detail the progress and some of the conflict, the positive and negative charge behind it all.

The Pipes narrative that day ran at a comfortable pace, and you had to pay attention to how he interchanged words; for example, "beans" could also mean money, and men and women became "cats and kitties." As you listened, you became amazed at how quick you could translate his message, and it gave you a feeling of accomplishment. That you could follow what was being said and it engaged the mind. You had the code.

No recording of what the Pipe put down that day exists. I've checked it out several times. I've learned also that I'm not the only one making the request. There've been enough requests to generate a form letter to the effect that no recording of what was said exists.

I believe them, but what does exist is the anthology – the *Good Wood* album on tape, and I have that. There is no narrative or background noise – just the tunes. The narrative of that day is lost, in a way making the album incomplete.

On stage, Pipe broke it down this way. There was England and across the ocean the Eastern Seaboard of North America – New England and their buddy cats, the South. Then went on to rap about a play in three acts, the *Sugar Act, Stamp Act* and *Townsend Act,* produced by England, a play that New England and their buddy cats didn't dig at all. This built up over the next sixteen years, and boom! - 1770, the "The Beantown Boil Over" – the Boston Massacre. Five years down the road from that, Patrick Henry gave his position on liberty or death, and Paul Revere was letting everyone know who was coming to town.

So in 1776, it turned into a situation where this street gang on the Eastern Seaboard of North America, the "Colonials," took on the "Red Coats" from England over turf. Now, over in Europe, the Red Coats were known for busting heads. They had a reputation. And this reputation was heading for a situation where the attitude held by the Colonials was, 'This isn't Europe.'

They were able to take the rumble, with George Washington on the ground, John Paul Jones on the water, and a supporting cast of thousands, to the point where seven years later, in 1783, they got a treaty inked in Paris, France to their liking. All the turf issues were settled.

I have to tell you that, as Pipe rapped on, he's the only person I ever saw who could pull off smoking in a museum. He effortlessly lit one right after another in such a manner that the habit became essential to his narrative. In short, it went unnoticed at the time, something you only became aware of long after the fact. As he smoked on, he rapped about the "library dividend," laying down in the "Week of Years" (1776 – 1783); the Colonials, aside from rumbling in the streets and forests with the Red Coats also set up and wrote down a lot of things – the direct result of literacy.

Made it a point to bring to the surface the setup of The First Continental Congress, where they wrote down the *Declaration of Independence* and the *Articles of Confederation.* In fact, these cats set up a bank, the Bank of North America, two years before the treaty was inked in Paris. All this was done before they signed. They didn't waste any time setting up the big experiment.

After the treaty, these cats came up with the *Northwest Ordinance* and opened up the land; everybody had something going, everybody was in business. Wrote down the *Bill of Rights* and opened the first government building – a mint.

And during this time a society evolved that could hold mencame from God or men came from monkeys. Demonstrating more than one view could be held in the same society, and relative order kept. Pipe making the point that the Forefathers were well aware - that in the past, in the present, and in future, it's man's nature to act like both—God and monkey.

With that said, Pipe crushed a smoke in an over-filled ash tray and let the lights fall on the *Big Notes,* and in the dark, blew the Tube. What followed were the best tunes I ever caught. The best licks and lyrics I ever heard.

The two new cuts on *Good Wood,* whose titles I won't give,take Beaufort to a whole new dimension. I know their titles, but I'm not giving them. The reason I'm not giving titles is thatif I bring them up and run into someone who knows them, I'll know a little something about them, and they'll know a little something about me. They'll be somebody who would either have something I want or connect me to someone who has whatI want, the actual album.

******

Like I said upfront, what I've given you is a paraphrase. Tofeel the total impact of Stovepipe, you had to be there that one afternoon. You had to catch the benchmarks of the exhibits he wrote and produced to understand, starting with the library and ending with the radio. And what I've given you here is a small part of that afternoon; in reality, I could talk about that afternoon for the next one hundred years and still not finish.

And all that I've done, I haven't done this alone. The woman from the coffee shop – I ran into her again. We were finally on the same page. The conversation went a little better, and with a shared obsession, we married about two hours after our second meeting.

She has actually rapped with the Pipe, been with the Pipe. And she'll tell you that the museum was the ultimate 'according to Stovepipe.' Of all the places he ever played, maybe the place to go out. She's told me he felt the impact of Beaufort would be like the circulating library - not felt for another hundred or so years. She's always reminding me I caught the last act. Last vinyl.

To date, we hold some fine artifacts. The best being the 1963 Comet, the years and cash outlay at times unbearable to talk about; the Comet with the reel-to-reel Wollensak in the backseat. We even have the invoice that matches the serial number on the tape recorder. It's signed "Stovepipe," no first name. I can also tell you the Tube and its case, along with the Acoustical 'A' Bomb, are in the works.

The Stovepipe resurrection has drawn me in. I know I'm on someone's radar, because of what I have. Probably in the range of some others too. There are some out there who think I ran the nine-word ad. I didn't. Here's the difference between who ran the ad and me - they want all the albums - I just want one. I also know what I have can easily be duplicated, I'm not the only one who can come up with a red and white '63 Comet, Wollensak tape recorder, photos, and tapes. The only things that can't be counterfeited are the albums. I only want one, the *Good Wood* album. The Whitman Sampler of Stovepipe'swork.

Who's The Rib? Did he blow out on a bus? Is he dead? There are more questions than answers. He's hard to calculate.

I do know this. People are starting to write and read about him. Seems everyone wants something from him – dead or alive. Like a first name, where does he really come from, and what'she really all about.

Prologue to the Compact Disc

Information on the six vinyl albums reside in the NogwickFiles found in our Record Data. Information on the one CD resides in our Mail Data. This is an important point of departure in the investigation. Mail Data is integrated data from all email sources and is less stable than the linear Report Data.

We continue to try to make the connection from some emails, where the writer claims to be Stovepipe, to our unidentified person, who claims to be 'awake.' However, so far, the connection can't be made. It looks like there should bea fit, an alignment, but there isn't. The integrated data can't provide enough information to prove our unidentified person and the person making the claim are the same.

The integrated Mail Data from one targeted computer leadsus to believe we have a person who plays the role of either imposter or informer. Someone is presenting a script written by the one who is "awake." We believe this person is more like the Radio Ventriloquist or Radio Voice, maybe the Rib.

Here, the integrated data fits a pattern found in the linear Nogwick Files, where Stovepipe is explained through the radio airwaves, magnetic tape and now electronic email. The pattern found in the Nogwick Files would suggest just as he was around the radio tape recorder, he's around these emails, around the person writing them.

From the analysis of ten primary emails, we know the seventh album is called by two names, *Pipe Reloaded* or *Bloodstream* and is a CD. Whether it is the one made in 1975 or a new CD, we can't determine.

The staff has been deployed to the regions. As expected, the Northeast region has the most activity. Book has made the most claims. The two I put on him are reporting what Book says he has and actually has may, be two different things. The high probability for results from him fading, but not out of view. They haven't completed their report, but initial reports show him not to be as promising as once thought.

The compilation data from the ten primary emails from the targeted computer have been integrated into a method to present the information in a narrative form, like the information presented in the Nogwick files. It's an attempt to present all the information on the seven albums in the same format. The seventh album is not part of the recorded oral history.

What is important to remember is the source of information for the first six albums is different than the source for the seventh and last album.

Album 7: Pipe Reloaded/Bloodstream (According to?)

Want to know about me? Let's turn on the light years so you can see. Let's put it on in April when the Big Dipper hangs upside down in outer space and pours out the meteors. It's a big month for meteors – meteors, here and gone in no time.

In this light, if you follow the curve of the handle on the Big Dipper, you'll run into two stars, Arcturus and Spica. If these two light bulbs blew on the day you made the big slide down the canal, you wouldn't know about Arcturus until your thirty-seventh birthday. And you'd never know about Spica unless you live to the age of 268. That's how long it takes the light from these bulbs to hit the floor of this crazy swinging sphere.

I only bring it up because tunes are the same way. In fact, in the musical universe, there are meteors, comets and stars forevery tune ever made. It's a big galaxy. Each gives off its ownlight. And in the case of tunes, what's reaching you now mightbe like the light from a bulb that blew several years before. I'vebeen living large on tunes I made forty years ago.

I'm not going to get into a long-winded rap about influences—classical, jazz, country, rock, pop, rhythm and blues—except to say they exist like the stars. Each is in its own constellation. The influences, like the constellations aren'tequal, just different. Each owns a part of the galaxy. Each givesa direction. Each has its story.

There's a whole universe of musical influence. And don't take it as a coincidence that there are eighty-eight known constellations and eighty-eight keys on the piano. These musical constellations are the keyboards behind each influence. And every once in a while, a cat goes out into space and plays the constellation keyboard, and a new star pops up.

See, voice and instruments are the planetariums and telescopes in this universe. The lens is always ground to have the power to catch a new star, a new audience. Dig! Each of these constellations has its own bucket of light years, and whendumped, each reaches us at different times, like the light from Arcturus and Spica. I know the audience for my new tunes is forty years down the road.

Yeah, they'll catch on just about three years after we realize Arcturus burned out. By that time, the chronologists will be eighty-plus years old or dead. Then, with what I have now, there'll be new ones. There'll be a mixture of past and presentthat will synthesize to the future chronologists. Be a gas to see how they all put it down, how it all turns out in the end. Just want to let you know up front that there's a little myth in all history. History is never pure. It moves in two gears, real and imagined. It comes in three colors: black, white, and gray. Later on, I'll get back to this.

******

Let me point out to the chronologist - I'm not dead, although I can be if there's a huge benefit in remaining dead. I'm just gone, been gone since the museum. I found a place that worked out absolutely perfect. After the museum, I tumbled into a lot of rolling hills covered with trees and valleyswith winding water. Have a few neighbors and a town up the road. And as much as I'd like to give you the name of the place,I won't. It's in Ohio if that helps. Won't tell you where I'm from - just where I'm at.

Fairly toned down from the early days, and I can rememberbeing a ton on a bus on my way to see someone I was involvedwith, so sick I wished I could die. All brought on by my outside curses. I admit, at the time, I liked everything out there. You name it, I took it. I've wrestled a lot of demons. Anyway, it must have been a pretty convincing show. I did pass out and I did touch the other side. Saw Jesus and all twelve of his disciples.

But what no cat caught was I made it to the next stop. I always put on a good show, even if I don't mean to. Heard the rumors and decided to go with it; a lot of cats think I'm dead, 'bus dead.' Found a place and settled in where I could concentrate on how to put my thumbprint on time. I didn't die.I just stopped and got off at Beaufort Boulevard to drop off what I picked up on the other side.

What I'm putting down is true – go to the Aces and Eights - see if I've played through. I know who's talking to the chronologists. Believe me, I know those who write and rap - who think they have the whole story when they only have a part. Half the time, they don't know what gear they're in. I'vetalked to a lot cats over time, tried to keep it at ten or less and move on. I've been around for a while and did this a lot. I've created a little history. I know who's out there.

But after a while, the whole scene became like water, and I felt myself sinking. Never could swim. Putting the art down infront of just five cats was pulling me under. I had a rumor I could play. So I connected to this place and people and gave itsome time.

About the only thing I'd let the chronologists get away withis, up to now, I've been dormant, not dead – big difference.

You know? Like a volcano. And that's about to change. I'm ready to explode. I got a CD coming out – my first one, the first one ever, and it's a new game. Let's see what they do with this.

I know who's talking to the Chronologists and the First

Contacts. In fact, I think I know who the Chronologists are.

******

Now, I'll admit to riding the four-stripe snake with Spoon. And I did a few bus stops with Noose. Did some repairs with Motor, some time with Dart and crossed the border with Boat, know them all. I don't know Book. But I do know his wife.

That's all clean. This rap that it all took place or ads up to twenty-four hours with each is bogus. It's their twist, not mine. It had to be more than a day. I can catch all of them in my wig, and it seems, at the very least, the measuring stick should be in days instead of hours.

It had to be days. Back then, I was releasing and that took some time. They make it sound like I'm some sort of meteor that blew across their wig. Some type of short impact cat that leaves a big crater, with everyone digging the crater instead of the meteor.

I'm a star. And I don't mean it like it sounds. What I mean is you have to look out into space to find me. The light I throw takes some time to hit you – more time than they're talking about. So I'm not buying it. It's more myth than truth.

They all saw me like I see the world. I see everything in black and white, with shades of gray. I like these three colors; they're truthful. I see other colors, but I stick with these. I'm a black and white movie in Technicolor.

Tell you another thing. Back then, there was a *Rib* behind every album, all with dark hair and eyes, except one. She had green eyes. No, make it two. One had light auburn hair. Each gave birth to Beaufort. Would have married any one of them but married none, married after *Good Wood*. Five are still around; one crossed over Jordan. I learned something good from each of them.

Learned there are only two true populations that count, male and female, who listen. Listen, not hear – big difference. You don't really hear tunes – you listen to them. Animals hear, people listen. And I'll tell you about my relationships with the women – not what you want to hear, but what you need to listen to.

And what bubbles to the surface is time – the time spent with each of them. And it was a strange time where we were emotionally together and usually physically apart, dependent on the written word or telephone. And in this set-up a cat has more time to think about what to say, even if it comes out all wrong once he says it.

Back then, you watched the mailbox and listened for the telephone. It was different from now. There was more power behind what was written and spoken because it wasn't instant. Every one of them knew how to write and how to talk to me. Every one of them gave me that time.

And the time given was filled with our thoughts. If you're a man, don't think you can't learn from a woman, and if you're a woman, don't think you can't learn from a man. There is no weaker sex. I'll put this on the table: I got six albums out there, and a CD on the way, and everyone that digs me understands cohabitation and collaboration.

I'll tell you this much - what happens over time when one hangs with another develops into a relationship, and they come in two flavors: good and bad. And they can travel in two directions, from bad to good and good to bad, and they'll bounce back and forth at the drop of a hat.

And in every relationship, somewhere in between good and bad and bad and good, you run into sex and have a few emotional collisions where sometimes there are no survivors. With sex comes commitment, unless you're like the monkeys at the zoo and have no cares who you do it in front of or who you do it to. When it hits that point with humans, evolution has either stopped or is reversing itself – that's why commitment is important. Commitment is the biggest component of evolution. It's what everyone wants but not what everyone gets.

******

Noose got it mostly right in what he puts down about *Bagpipes and Bongos.* How God shorted man a rib and made a woman, side A and side B. The female sex and the male sex, and from the two populations, there is "connected" sex when we're joined, when one enters another. When we become one, when we're neither female nor male, and this connection is probably when we're the closest to feeling like God since God is both. And if God isn't both, God's neither.

If God wasn't both, he wouldn't have created us this way and set it up this way. That's why we get off on that brief feeling. And I don't know who or what God is, but the closest

I can come to what it must feel like to be God is the orgasm everyone is after that comes from this connection.

The true feeling from the connection can only happen front to front and not front to rear or anyplace else, even though this happens – all I'm going to say on that. And there is a price, and it can only be paid in commitment. Otherwise, it loses its value and becomes cheap.

Noose did a fair job in what he put on you cats about the only Rib directly rapped about. Won't give her name, but will put on you that the way she was at the time, I could believe God was a woman. Like God, she was always good to me. We had balance, the best sound each could make in *Bagpipes and Bongos*. Probably the only big change I've made since then – that God is both or neither, but not a woman. Can also tell you we connected not long after we met, and she orbits around my mind every day.

But the day I picked up Spoon, heading north out of Athens, and I let *Save Your Strength* out of the bag, I was in the autumn of a relationship full of color and connection. Enough to hold your thoughts through most of the winter until it got too gray and cold. When this happened, there was no way two could keep it warm.

If you want to know more about *Save Your Strength*, maybe I can clear some things up because I'd be lying if I told you I was the only one behind it. And I know the controversy concerning the *Big Notes* and me and who really did it. You want to know who played all the instruments? She did.

It's in your cats' human nature to always be thinking musical instruments, but there are other instruments out there to be played, and she was very instrumental in a lot ways. She was dark-haired and dark-eyed with a body that had a strong gravitational pull. But more than that, she got me to finish a lot of things I started. The only thing she ever finished was the relationship.

And if pain can be positive, a lot got done to take my mind off her. Can tell you we were pretty young. She had black and white striped walls in her bedroom and there isn't a constellation out there that doesn't remind me of her and the direction she gave me, the course she put me on.

When I dropped *Sticks to Bricks* on Boat, there was no doubt I troubled him with all he had going on and the way I did it. How he wanted to change. Especially when he broke my 'Calhoun' with the C notes he was carrying, could see it in his eyes. I got a lot on Boat, and I've heard what he has on me. And I wasn't a stranger to the weight he was carrying. I had my own bundle.

We had a lot in common that we never rapped about. I had someone I was writing all those tunes not "for" - but "to." There's a difference that I won't go into now. In fact, out of all of the Ribs, I could go on about her the most, a divorced working mother. And dig how fate works because in the beginning, I sure wasn't looking for her, but in the end, that was all I did.

Here's what Boat and I had in common that he never knew about. I'd also known her for years. And men were attracted to her shape, dark eyes, and dark hair and I never thought I'd be one, but I was. I was always in her corner.

I'll let you judge how it turned out and how far it went. Tell you this much, I not only wrote to her, I gave, built, fixed things, took in her cat and named my bike after her.

The attraction wasn't all physical. Her beauty was in her heart. Like Boat, before it started, I knew all she'd been through. I wanted to take care of her and her family. Over the years, my admiration for her grew slowly and developed a deep root.

She was smart and worked hard. She used to like to run up and down the hills of a cemetery, and the men, women and children under the headstones missed her on the days she didn't come. She brought what they had lost – life – that's how she was.

And if I hadn't been committed at the time, it would all be different today. We severely tested each other. All I got out of it was a blanket and, a bottle of wine, some glasses and a hat, that I have to this day and always will. Like the Mounties, she sent me back to where I belonged. Every direction I took with the tunes on that album came from her compass, her heart; it's one of my strongest.

And by the time I was in Fairfield County, upstairs in the can with Dart, I came out with *Radio Ventriloquist.* Then, just about everything in my life was underground, and I did it so well that I was starting to be imitated above ground. Dart didn't have to tell me; I knew. The Rib behind the album made it thatway.

She came after me, and I was flattered and single. She was determined and married. She didn't have dark hair, but she didhave dark eyes. As much as I tried to fight the chemistry, she and I connected to a potion that couldn't be overcome. And if I felt anything, it was desire. The desire she had for me.

At the time, I was against everything established, andmarriage was at the front of the list. I've been down the road with a married woman, so have a lot of cats, and everyone willtell you the scenery is great, but the road is rough, double rough. And those collisions with no survivors I mentioned earlier? Well, she'd be one of them.

Found out about it the day I got out. She crossed Jordan onenight using my heart as a bridge, and it broke under the weight.She went by her own hand, the hand I used to hold. And here's where the tragedy comes in. At the time, I was so undergroundthere wasn't a soul I could rap to about it. Maybe, Dart, there was something about him, but he got out a day early.

To this day, on clear nights, I try to find her star. I'll know it by the light it gives off, and I hope it burns better and brighter than it did down here.

And if you think I learned anything from that, you'd be dead wrong. Let me tell you about the road conditions at the time of *Atomic Peanut* and the mushroom cloud I was flying through. Like the '63 Comet, I was real close to burning out somewhere down the road. In fact, I was running out of road - out of motivation. I needed a mechanic after I met this Rib.

I met her in a bar, and she had everything I needed: dark hair, dark eyes and the only words to describe her would be striking or stunning, another divorced mother. She was a student nurse. She could've been on any calendar. She was a pin-up. I described her once to Motor, but he and his buddy Ernie had no idea; they were thinking Miss America 1950.

We took up with each other for a long time; we had a pretty strong connection. And at the end of my days with the Mounties, after I got caught in the wind and found myself on the other side of the pond, continually fighting the heat, the rain, the insects, the rats, the infections, the crazy Asians – she wrote to me all the time.

I didn't mind backing up the country that gave the world Benjamin Franklin, Mark Twain and Will Rogers. Knowing what they said at times would get them shot in a lot of other countries. Anyway, she was always in contact. The biggest bombing campaign of the fracas couldn't stop her. I always got mail.

It all changed when I got back; changed for a lot of cats. Right before I got out, she met another guy. She married him.

Before it happened, I put up a fight, but it turned out like the war, which was full of surprises, and none of them were good. She tried to come back, but it never happened. And if it's any comfort to her, I know the location of her star, and I gaze at it from time to time.

I came up with *Good Wood* when I got right with a pairof green eyes. I met her in school. And if I learned anything from this Rib, it was respect. I tried every trick in the book to connect with her, but she was *Good Wood* and knew how to keep the flame going without that fuel. I came close on a lot ofoccasions, but that's it.

The concept of commitment came with this package, and I thought I was there, but the track record at the time was bad. It certainly didn't add any support. And if I could thank her for anything, it would be for all the great raps we had and all the near misses.

Tell you another thing about *Good Wood;* it came out like a pair of gloves in a winter coat or, better yet, like a five-dollarbill you find in an old pair of jeans. Cats caught it at the museum only because I was wearing those jeans. One more thing; not to confuse anyone, but all my relationships with the others were influenced by her. She was the first and has alwaysbeen part of my galaxy.

To be honest, these Ribs are like light years; each has her own distance from me, and their light hits me at different times and in different ways, no two alike. I know sequence is important in any history. To the Chronologists, all you have here is how the light is hitting me today, and that will change tomorrow.

And except for the one I hooked up with and who I won't go into, who overwhelmed the competition, I can remember the last time I saw each of them, the single, the divorced, and the married. I've pulled my hat trick of love. I loved every oneof them.

Spoon has it right when he puts on you cats that when I wasten, I was twenty, been many when ten was twenty, and twentywas thirty. I like the female flesh.

But only seven come up to the surface, the one I married and the six I knew. I played for their hearts instead of their bodies. And if we're flesh and spirit, I like the spirit even better. Each of them gave me something more than flesh. Like I said, I learned something good from each of them.

Now, I'm sorry if I gave a chronology you're not used to. Different from the first way it'll be put down and the way it'll probably get picked up. I wouldn't pay too much attention to it, but you can if you want. I'll also tell you this; I know this first chronology and the true chronology.

Won't apologize for the way I described the Ribs behind today's chronology. The first cold hard fact is the strongest in the herd are usually the best looking. In the herd of females andmales, the law of attraction is based on how you carry your weight, mentally and physically. You're at the mercy of the gene pool and your own self-discipline. If that weren't the case, weight control wouldn't be the industry it is today with all its equipment and pills.

The second cold hard fact is you only get to be the strongestfor a while. It's not a permanent position. So everything changes over time. But I guess the point I'm trying to make in all of this is if there were no Ribs, there'd be no albums and nochronologists.

What was mentioned once doesn't mean it didn't happen over and over, just because it wasn't mentioned again and again. I'm telling you this because to go forward, you have to look back. Otherwise, cars wouldn't have rearview mirrors. It's always good to know what's behind you.

******

There's a melody in your wig, but you'll only know it by the lyrics you put behind it. You first catch the melody, then start singing the words. That's how a tune works. You listen toa melody to hear the words.

Melodies without lyrics are the most dangerous in capturing your imagination. You have to come up with your own lyrics; sometimes you can and sometimes you can't, but when you can, it makes all the difference.

Melodies and lyrics make the world spin. There isn't a culture that doesn't have both; everyone gets a tune. And a lotcan be said through a tune. It's human nature that if you have one, you'll want the other. If you have the melody, you'll want the words, you'll make them up. If you have the words, you'llmake up the melody.

I'll give you a case in point. Let's talk Beaufort and all who,one way or another, were behind each album. And what it was like being with the ones who gave birth to Beaufort. Lyrically, all I've said so far could have also been told in thirty-six linesbroken down into nine stanzas.

Let's take a case where I give you some lyrics, and you findthe melody. Let's make a tune. Here's my half, the lyrics; yourhalf will be the melody. There's one playing in your head already, when you connect, when this happens, the tune you come up with will be the same as what the tube told the instruments to wrap around the words. Your melody and minewill be the same. Let's look at what

I've told you so far, by lineand stanza: ***On the Way to Beaufort.***

One night with my bus station bottle on the Beaufort side oftown

That's where she found me; that's where she tracked me down

Well it'd been a slingshot kind of affair - ya see

She could pull me back, she could launch me.

And even though she was fair and kind

With a head like a rock, I had something else in mind

Yeah, right from the kickoff, I had the wrong offense.

Right from the tip-off, she had the right defense.

Oh, she was fluent in love's splendid tongue

I've been down the road; I've had my bell rung

Yeah, we played on a short field, love's wild game.

She got wounded, I pulled up lame

And we were both even at the start

I was quick – she was smart

But I thought we put it all to rest

And when she found me – I was far from my best

A smoke dangling from my chops

A ride in the parking lot waiting for the cops

She'd come close to falling over the edge

She hadn't forgotten love's crumbling ledge

Yeah, and all the time she was on the right track

But I reached out – I pulled her back

And where I became her permanent scar

She became my exploding cigar

She wanted to talk about love's critical mass

All I could talk about was my half-empty glass

She wailed on about her heart, covered with bad tattoos

I just looked at her, hoping for some better news

Well, it never came and here's my advice

Sometimes it's better to sacrifice

All that you have and all that you know

And make love your friend and not your foe

Take what she gives, and give what she'll take.

Anything less would be a mistake

Don't go there, don't have her track you down

Don't be found on the Beaufort side of town

What I'm giving you here is all in a tune on the CD I've made. Here's the lyrics. You'll know the melody behind them when you hear it. It will be just as you imagined. This is a smalltaste of what's coming.

******

So Dig! I've given all you cats something you wanted to know. I've answered some questions. But the only thing you really need to know is those albums I made light years ago havea lot of spirit and flesh behind them. Maybe they are my kids. Do I have any kids? I'll let you guess. Someday, you'll find out, but not today. I'll only tell you there's new spirit and flesh behind what's coming. Check your rearview mirror.

I'll also put on you that what I've put down and made – figuratively and literally - has been picked up and bought by alot of cats for a lot of years. I live in their heads vacation in their pockets. I've sold a lot and got a lot.

Am I satisfied? Well, I'll tell you what, like everything else, satisfaction comes and goes. You get on any big four-striped snake and read the bumpers; you'll see what I mean. Bumper stickers can tell you a lot. Bumper stickers are the bedrock of American literature. I've seen them on the right, on the left andin the middle, and they cover it all—religion, politics, and sex, right up to the obvious—"shit happens."

You read them, and you know the kind of tunes being played in front of your windshield. So, I guess I'm as satisfiedor dissatisfied as the guy in front of me. Depends on how muchI buy into what his bumper is saying. Saw one the other day I could buy into – "a moment of silence for Marcel Marceau."

Can also tell you bumper sticker attitude is the good and bad brother of satisfaction. As far as attitude is concerned, I've been around both brothers, and they've taken me to some goodand bad places. And it's not that my attitude can't get me any satisfaction; it's that it can't get me enough. Remember puttingthis rap on some skinny cat from England when I was studyingeconomics over there a long time ago, and he ran with it.

If we have total satisfaction, we wouldn't need the word "attitude." And that's what that cat was all about – attitude. Hewas dissatisfied, and at the time, so was I. But the one thing about attitude is it always changes, depending on which brother you're hanging with.

To tell you the truth, it's been more like some episode of Marlin Perkins' *Wild Kingdom,* brought to you by Mutual of Omaha Insurance. Letting you think a little insurance might be a good idea after showing you all the snakes, gators, rats and cats that could come after you. Where I've been cast as one of the higher primates and how I've evolved from what I was forty years ago when that show was popular to what I am today.

Tell you the nature of putting down the Beaufort, to where it can survive, has had its costs. Some things that were once part of me have been devoured.

I keep a lot of things under my hood to get me down the road. I even have insurance now. I've made a lot of stops. I learned a lot, especially from higher education, only it wasn't in the classroom but at the bookstore. Found out in this deal it was far better to be the seller than the buyer. Anybody that's been to college knows what I'm talking about. Everyone has their own story about the bookstore.

The professors, publishers and stores know what's in print has almost limitless worth, and what's out of print is worthless. You bought the first edition in the beginning of the term, and by the end of the term, it's been replaced by the second edition. They manipulate the student market so the student always buys high and sells low, really low.

The college bookstore is the model for excessive executive compensation. Students are a trapped market, a can't-miss market.

Is the setup right? Is it wrong? I'll go as far as to say it exists, that it's an education in itself and that I own more than one. It's all part of the package, all part of the insurance, all part of the Beaufort.

Take you down the road a little further. It doesn't end with the bookstores, which cost me the Comet, the ride that took me to all my gigs, the ride that stopped here, there and everywhere, the Comet and everything inside it.

At a lot of those stops, there was one machine that always held a lot of coin. That one machine was always found in two rooms: the men's room and the women's room.

Any machine that has the sex drive behind it is going to generate cash. This is just another way of telling you I also own a vending company that services the needs of these two rooms. The company cost me some pictures. Someday, I'll buy it all back, Comet and all, and that day is getting closer.

Yeah, I've got a lot of machines spotted in the bars near large campuses and truck stops across the country. Won't give you the name of the business, but will tell you it's an interesting business and right up there with the bookstores. In fact, some years it makes more.

You want another First Contact? My man Machine takes care of them, and here's what I've learned from him. In this business, to hit gold, you have to understand the two true populations.

In the room for the one population, one fills the machine to capacity, when the coin goes in, the raincoat better come out. If it doesn't, the next move is collaring some bartender about the coin lost.

Eventually, it escalates into a lot of turned-over tables, chairs and broken glass, not to mention the spillage. But more important, you short the buyer in this room, and it might not happen that night, but one night, the machine is coming off thewall. The people from this population won't forget all the physical pleasure the machine shorted them. So you keep the machine in this room full.

With the other population, you fill every other slot. The odds of collaring the barkeep are along the same line as a tossed coin landing on its edge, not saying it can't happen, just giving you the odds. With this population, if they're that interested, they'll try again, paying double for what they want. If they're that interested, they'll play two slots.

Why? Because they're in touch with their emotions. If youshort them, they're not going to make it public information. Actually, you short them, and you might be saving them from some excessive emotional baggage. So, in this setup, the machines are at fifty percent capacity, yet they cash in at a onehundred percent.

Like I said, over time, some parts of me have been devoured. I'm beyond good and bad and deal with what exists.My enterprises are like fire and water; they exist as things thatcan do both – good and bad. That's how I am now. I'm also one who wants to leave my thumbprint on time, the Beaufort. My enterprises exist because of this and this only.

******

You want another contact? I've got a cat I call Bit, and there isn't anything the computer can throw or the Internet can kickhe can't catch. Whatever is out there, he can pull it down and run with it, better and farther than anyone out there. He's no twenty-four-hour cat. In fact, neither is Machine.

Bit understands Al Gore didn't invent the Internet – pornography did. Let's see if we can't get something good out of something bad. That's what Bit holds in his wig.

I'd be lying if I put on you cats that I don't feel a little like Uncle Albert and Uncle John watching ten inches of vinyl dressed in a cardboard jacket turn into the compact disc living inside a plastic case. I've learned as you get older, the effort you put into anything takes longer, and you can't pick it up like use to.

But the burning rates have changed. The Beaufort has been computerized, has its own font, its own keyboard, and has probably fifteen functions within the program. I have the only package, and it lives on only one computer with backup memory sticks in a safety deposit box at a bank in Ohio. It's gone from something written to something programmed. It's evolved from when I burned my first disc.

Here's the deal. Right now, I have the warhead, a CD coming straight from this program. I'm working on the delivery system. It's called *Pipe Reloaded* or *Bloodstream (Bloodstream* - one word, not two). I like both, so I call it both. This is my way of making up for no more Side A and B on the LP.

Everything from here on out will have two titles – A and B. The way you hear the tunes will let you decide which title you like better – A or B. You decide what to call it. Either way, I'll know what you are talking about. I know this approach might add some confusion for the future chronologists. There'll be more albums.

I won't make it easy; I want to put it out there so that if you catch it - you'll catch it like a light year. Want it to travel by word of mouth to your universe - look here, look there, do this, do that, go here, go there.

Make one travel the galaxy of their mind to get where I am. Want it so one has to do some work to catch the light I'm throwing, and in the end, put down the experience was well worth it. Have to think on it. Right now, I got to get back to someone; I got a plane to catch.

Epilogue

Now you know as much as we do and more than the Chronologists. Thurston Nogwick has yet to forward his files. Over the years, my staff and I have been solid anticipating the cost required in capturing the artifacts we're after. No one has been solid anticipating the cost of the nine-word offer: 'Any record albums…Made by Stovepipe…Name your price.' We're beginning to wonder if a price can be named. It's a concern. The nine-word offer; something we've never faced. All we know is how much we've put into the project.

But the nine-word offer did lead to seven albums. At times, we believe these albums are like the Lost City of Gold or the Fountain of Youth; they only exist in people's imagination. But most of the time, we feel both artists and albums are waiting to be found, like The Lost City of Gold and The Fountain of Youth.

We're at war with our beliefs and feelings. Our feelings are winning. We don't know what to believe. The project brought on by the offer will prove us to be either wise men or fools. Probably the only reason we continue is we want to know which.

We still hold to our theory on the Chronologists. It's been filled in by the concept of producing the best sound from any voice instrument through Beaufort, the 'New Notation.' The Beaufort and *New Notation* are similar to the Bible and The *New Testament* and the changes brought on by their discovery.

We can see, from what we know, how the Chronologists could place him as the messiah between LP and CD and follow the model they've chosen. In Stovepipe, they have one who moves in mysterious ways, someone who spoke to small crowds many times. It's felt these small crowds are just now beginning to generate a larger audience.

We found his disciples in unlikely places—truck stops, busstops, gas stations, jails, boats and museums. The places we've all been. He had an impact on everyone who crossed his path, on every audience that ever heard him, he gave them an awareness of what is and isn't.

It's felt the Chronologist may have their boy for what they want to accomplish. The one who is 'awake' or our 'Electronic Voice,' if they are one and the same, they seem to be holding their own with Chronologists. It's felt once we find Stovepipe and tell him what we know about the Chronologists, we will probably be telling him something he already knows.

We've drawn some conclusions. First, Stovepipe isn't like Johnny Appleseed or Paul Bunyan, who turn up to be mostly myths. We believe he's beyond myth and more like D. B. Cooper or Big Foot. People saw D. B. get on and off the plane, but no one has seen him since; no one knows where he is. Like Big Foot, Pipe has been sighted but never captured. Stovepipe is like both or, better yet, like both rolled up into one.

At times, it feels we're on our way to the Lost City of Gold, The Fountain of Youth, looking for D.B. Cooper, Big Foot in the form of Stovepipe. The possibilities of finding Stovepipe seem severely limited, yet the search will continue. We've come to the conclusion we can't stop ourselves. I doubt our efforts will end in the last quarter as planned.

Neither Thurston Nogwick nor the Chronologist knows about the seventh album. After the compilation of the seventh album, we made the decision to strike first in our war of documentation with the Chronologists. We believe the seventh album will lead to the other six. We felt we found our hope in the sixth album, but it's the seventh we need to concentrate on.

We take the position it's a preemptive strike. The support we are after in our action is found in the fact our work, so far, is the first, not the final, documentation we believe the Chronologists would present to an unsuspecting public.

With what we give you, the wider net has been thrown. We, now, like the Chronologists, know what we're after. I want, we want, to put these seven albums right next to some of the artifacts we already have, right next to: the lighter, shoes, microphone, camera, key, belt, cufflinks, starter pistols, cars, bike, necktie and gavel. I want, we want, all the artifacts, all the moments the Boomers have known. The only thing we can't afford is to overlook any moment in our time that changed us. Don't forget…4563Boomer.com.

www.ingramcontent.com/pod-product-compliance
Lightning Source LLC
Chambersburg PA
CBHW041055310726
48978CB00011BA/565